Family Life:

A Biblical Perspective

by
L.A. Stauffer

10 Digit ISBN   1-58427-179-5
13 Digit ISBN 978-158427179-6

Guardian of Truth Foundation
P.O. Box 9670
Bowling Green, Kentucky 42102
1-800-428-0121
www.truthbooks.net

Table of Contents

Introduction

This book is not just another book about the home. It is a unique book, being both instructive and practical, written by a Christian who is both well versed in the doctrine and successful in his practice of it. It will be helpful to people who are willing to be taught this subject by God and His Word.

The title suggests the context in which brother Stauffer's comments are made. He continually appeals to what the Bible says. His teaching is neither sociological or psychological. At best he would be an amateur in these fields; but from the viewpoint of biblical instruction he is a professional.

Brother Stauffer's intention is to help people as did our Lord Jesus. He understands the biblical concept of happiness. The goal of his instruction is to help prepare people to enjoy eternal happiness while at the same time seeking to help them to "love life and see good days."

The author clearly understands that morality in all human relationships springs from creation rather than Christianity. He reasons that men have moral duties because each is made in God's image. The response to this fact is the duty to live a moral life. Life lived on a moral plain, as devised by God, will produce happy results.

The author teaches principles first and then discusses their practical application. His style of writing makes abstract concepts come alive. He puts his words together in an interesting manner so that his thoughts can be understood as well as easily remembered.

This book addresses the hard questions; it doesn't avoid them. The questions and answers are set in a modern time and present situations. He is both forthright and fair. He is both sympathetic and caring. As a concerned Christian he brings the truth to bear upon human frailties and fleshly temptations.

As one reasons with brother Stauffer one soon realizes that he is studying with a mature Christian, a seasoned preacher, and an experienced husband and father. In striving to build strong faith the author supplies more than cold and academic propositions. His teaching is warmed by the reminder that the inspired instruction comes from the person of the Holy Spirit. He encourages the Christian by reminding him that he is empowered to live through the Spirit's influence coming through inspired testimony. This is a most important point.

I recommend this material; and I do it heartily. It is scriptural, sensible, and sane. It will help the married as well as the unmarried. Brother Stauffer's comments are made within "the biblical perspective."

Harry Pickup, Jr.

November 1988

Biblical Perspective

Introduction

Pope John Paul II saw clearly a microcosm of American life when he recently visited the United States and faced a host of angry parishioners. John Paul is recognized as the head of the Catholic Church, alleged to be a successor of the apostle Peter, and supposed to give infallible direction to his people. He found, however, that American Catholics are in no mood to be told what they can and cannot do. The people are determined to define the beliefs of their church and are stiff-necked about their rights. The Catholic Church in America is teetering on the brink of anarchy or, if not that, attempting to move in the direction of democracy.

Catholics, for example, demand the right for priests to marry, for women to be priests, to use birth control, to seek abortions, to be homosexuals, and, in short, the right to defy the authority of the church — the pope himself. When these demands are met — if they are — new ones will be championed. These demands are but symptoms of the real problem. The Catholic Church is facing a crisis of authority. Whether right or wrong, the people insist that they have a say. What is happening in Catholicism, however, is typical of American society in general.

The citizens of these United States daily move nearer and nearer to demands for absolute freedom. Fellow Americans cry out for abortion on demand, freedom of press for pornographers and filth purveyors, co-ed dormitories where teenagers openly live together, rights of homosexuals to display publicly perverted life-styles, easy divorce that allows parents to walk off from family responsibilities, legalizing of drugs that destroy lives and minds, murder of older folks who are no longer deemed useful to society, and who knows what next. Somewhere in the scramble for rights and freedom, the idea of authority and responsibility has been lost and fewer and fewer Americans are inclined to search for them.

What is happening, fellow Americans? The "land of the free and home of the brave" faces, as does Catholicism, a crisis of authority. Citizens of this great nation crave unrestrained freedom. No one wants to be told what to do. Auto workers ask for more money, but have little interest in submitting to their employer or in the responsibility to make a good automobile. Business men or women lust for unbridled sex and could not care less whose wife or husband is their partner. TV evangelists solicit unlimited support for their programs with no conscience about deception or devouring the living of widows to obtain it. Politicians seek both respect and votes, but with greedy eyes unscrupulously pass laws to benefit those who will grease their palms. What happened to honest, fair, responsible, law-abiding citizens?

These qualities were pushed off into the wings with "you" when *"I"* moved center stage. Only when it is understood how *"I"* revised the script to produce a dramatic soliloquy will it be clear why a cast is no longer needed except as props. But why have *"I"* become number one and why do *"I"* no longer care about numbers two or three or four — whether it be my wife, my husband, my children, my neighbors, my fellow workers? The answer to this is alarmingly simple! A breakdown has occurred in family life.

Other than the individual, the oldest, the smallest, the closest, and the most basic unit of society is the family. Families, therefore, form the building blocks of a community, a nation, a civilization. As families go, so go the city, the country, and the world. When, for example, love, respect, honesty, responsibility, subjection, fairness — the bonding elements of the family — are not taught in the home, how can they possibly exist in society? No nation can long survive the absence of these fundamentals in family life; they are the basis of all human relationships.

To be specific, when teenage rebellion or juvenile delinquency is prevalent in a nation, respect for authority and for others is not being inculcated in the home. Immorality, greed, divorce, and crime in cities reflect a lack of training and discipline in the lowest level of society — the family. When lying, cheating, and dishonesty dominate the business world, basic absolutes have not been instilled at the knee of a father and in the arms of a mother. Although both government and the church must enforce and teach these fundamentals, the role of the family is primary. But what has happened to the family? Why is it failing so miserably?

Failure of the Home
1. Abdicated. It has failed, number one, because it has abdicated! Fathers and mothers are no longer teaching, training, and disciplining their children. Fathers in the grip of greed are spending longer hours at work, in the lust for pleasure are devoting themselves to golf or bowling, and in the ease of leisure are planting themselves silently before the TV. Mothers have opted for careers to satisfy inflated egos, filled their minds with the distortions of "soaps" and talk-show prattle, and decided that housewiving is demeaning and beneath their talents. Who, then, is in charge of the kids? Schools, churches, TV playwrights, the print media, and ill-informed friends are seeing to the education of the children.

2. Evolution. The home has failed, secondly, because it is infiltrated by an evil and corrupt philosophy that now dominates the media and the nation. Evolution, a philosophical and scientific theory, has attained respectability in this country within the past two generations. It controls many departments of instruction in the school systems, from elementary level to college. It is accepted by numerous religious denominations, promoted by many of the media, assumed by all branches of government, and undergirds most therapy and psychological treatment.

As a scientific theory evolution assumes that matter is eternal, that dead matter spontaneously gave birth to life, and that life developed naturalistically and orderly into the intelligent and complex forms of today. Man, therefore, the theory says, is merely the highest form of animal. He is simply a thinking ape or gorilla. If, of course, man is no more than an animal, why can he not follow his "instincts" to do as he pleases? Why cannot other humans be his prey — for sex, money, power? What prohibits him if he's the "fittest" from stepping center-stage? The scientific theory evolves into a philosophical theory.

3. Humanism. The philosophy of evolution is kin to the older theory of humanism and the two have joined forces to fight the theocentric view of past society. Both theories propose an anthropocentric universe in which all wisdom is presumed to originate *with* man *for* man. Man, thus, is left to himself to decide what is good, what is pleasurable, and what is beneficial (see Jer. 10:23; Prov. 14:12; Matt. 15:9; Col. 2:8). Ultimately, all things in the universe gravitate toward man, and more specifically toward *"me."* The result is a *"me"* generation that accepts no restraints.

Humanism, of course, did not originate with this country. It has existed since Adam and Eve who in effect said, "I want that fruit and I want it now!" Any time men disbelieve and forget God, as did the original pair, they fall into selfishness and every hurtful lust. When all men succumb to lust the family disintegrates, immorality prevails, and society decays. It happened to the world of Rome and for the same reason. They forgot God! Note the apostle Paul's description of that nation in the first century:

> For the invisible things of him since the creation of the world are clearly seen, being perceived through the things that are made, even his everlasting power and divinity; that they may be without excuse; because that, knowing God, *they glorified him not as God, neither gave thanks; but became vain in their reasoning, and their senseless heart was darkened. Professing themselves to be wise, they became fools, and changed the glory of the incorruptible God for the likeness of an image of corruptible man, and of birds, and four-footed beasts, and creeping things* (Rom. 1:20-23).

The apostle continues to describe how *"God gave them up in the lusts of their hearts unto uncleanness"* and *"gave them up unto vile passions"* (Rom. 1:24,26). The apostle then lists all the wickedness of that decaying civilization. When men forsake God for their own wills and pleasure, the foundation of society crumbles. When Paul later spoke of perilous times that were to come, he enumerated such things as *"lovers of self,"* *"lovers of money,"* *"disobedient to parents,"* *"without self-control,"* and *"lovers of pleasure rather than lovers of God"* (2 Tim. 3:1-5).

This book, as the title indicates, purports to be a study of family life from the viewpoint of the Bible. The writer believes that the biblical perspective of the home is what not only America but every society needs. When followed as the foundation of family life, it will create a healthy respect for authority, eliminate the "me generation," and inject the antidote of responsibility into a carefree people.

Three Premises
1. God is. Three premises form the basis of this study. One, God is (Heb. 11:6). *"The heavens declare the glory of God; And the firmament showeth his handiwork,"* the Psalmist says (Psa. 19:1). It is absurd in modern times to view the intricacies of life, the orderly arrangement of the universe, and the precision of nature's operations and deny the existence of an intelligent Creator behind it. As the Psalmist says elsewhere, *"The fool has said in his heart, There is no God"* (Psa. 14:1). The harder scientists try and the more they fail to turn up tangible evidence of materialistic

evolution, the more foolish man's rejection of God becomes.

2. Jesus — God's Son. Second, Jesus is God's Son (Jn. 20:30,31). A body of writings, known as the Bible, demonstrates by the evidence of prophecy that Jesus is the Messiah foretold in the Old Testament (*e.g.* Isa. 53; Psa. 22; Isa. 7:14; Mic. 5:2; Zech. 9:9). The Bible also contains the writings of competent, honest, contemporary witnesses who suffered and died for the testimony that Jesus was raised from the dead. They, without successful refutation or disproof, proclaimed immediately the resurrection of Christ at Jerusalem before the very officals who crucified him, buried him, and guarded his tomb (see Acts 2:1,22-36).

3. Bible — God's Word. Third, the Bible is the word of God (Eph. 3:1-5; 1 Cor. 2:6-13). The Bible is a library of 66 books written by some 30 or 40 men over a period of about 1500 years. The theme of sin, redemption, and a coming Savior supplies a unity that demands a superintending mind that guided all its writers. The writers claim that this mind was the mind of God. More than 2500 times they allude to the fact that God gave them this message (*e.g.* Isa. 1:2; Jer. 1:4). In short, evidence indicates: *"All scripture is given by inspiration of God"* (2 Tim. 3:16).

God's Marriage Manual

God, this study will affirm, is infinite in wisdom and perfectly qualified to counsel the human family on home life. It is, therefore, to his book man must turn for knowledge of the make-up and workings of family life. Women who want to make a dress secure a handbook on *Basic Sewing* and men who plan to work on a car obtain a manual on *Automotive Repair*. Who is more capable than God, the architect of the home, to author a manual on family life?

1. God Created Man. God created man, including male and female, in his own likeness (Gen. 1:26,27; 5:1). Having designed both man and woman, God in his infinite wisdom (Psa. 139) knows what is in the best interest of each. He knows how they can best function as husband and wife; he knows how they can best function as father and mother. He knows, furthermore, what the strengths and the needs of both the man and the woman are. He alone can infallibly dictate the relationship of the two together. Only those who can trust and follow Jehovah's will can experience the peace, the joy, the happiness God intended this relationship to produce.

2. God's Authority. The test for every man is whether he has the will to submit to God's authority. It is noted that even Christians are kicking over the traces, chafing at the bit, straining against the reins to free themselves from the Master's control. God as Creator has the right and the authority to direct the steps of man, his creation (Acts 17:24-29; Eph. 4:6). The solution to the problems of family life is to believe God, trust his will, yield to his control (Matt. 4:4,10; Acts 5:29).

3. God's Wisdom. The crisis of authority results, first, from a failure to believe in God's word. Are his teachings truth? Are they valid for modern life? Will they really work? The infinite wisdom and eternal purpose of God are being questioned when men of little faith doubt his plan for family life. When this is rejected by Christians the foundation of not only the home but their entire lives is destroyed (Matt. 7:21-28). Repudiation of God's rule stems, second, from a lack of will to curb lust (Lk. 9:23). The siren call of covetousness, as an example, lures housewives out of the home and into the work force when the spirit is not willing to subdue the lust for things (Gal. 5:16-18). So it is with a host of other desires that families refuse to suppress (see 1 Jn. 2:15-17).

Conclusion

The same crisis prevails in every phase of modern life. A Christian questions God's authority when he revolts against civil law that he just doesn't happen to like (see Rom. 13:1,2). The Lord's servant rebels against God when he resists the dictates of his employer because he thinks they are unfair (see Eph. 6:5-9). God's people challenge his authority when they retaliate against a neighbor who violates their rights (see Matt. 5:38-48). Disciples of Christ oppose God anytime they reject the instruction of the Master Teacher who has all authority in heaven and on earth (see Matt. 28:18; 10:24; Lk. 10:16).

Brethren must not, as Israel and Judah, become rebels against God and his law. Husbands, wives, fathers, mothers, children must all listen to the God who created them, believe that he knew what he was doing, and resolve to fulfill their roles in family life. This study is designed to help each one learn the place that God has assigned him or her in the home. May he help all to accept that place by faith.

An Outline Study Guide

Introduction:

A. List several demands made by Catholics._____

_____

B. Enumerate evils Americans seek and compare to Gal. 5:19-21 and 1 Cor. 6:9,10.

_____

C. What is the crisis that produces both of these?_____

_____

D. What does God say about man as an authority to himself (Jer. 10:23; Prov. 14:12; Matt. 15:9; Col. 2:8; Acts 5:29)?_____

_____

I. Failures of the Home:

A. Why have fathers failed?_____

Why have mothers failed?_____

B. What scientific theory dominates society?_____

What are its assumptions?_____

C. What philosophy is closely aligned with evolution?_____

_____

What do "theocentric" and "anthropocentric" mean?_____

_____

Define humanism:_____

_____

D. What first-century attitudes parallel modern views (Rom. 1:20-32; 2 Tim.

3:1-5)? _____

_____

II. Three Premises:

A. How does the Bible argue God's existence (Psa. 19:1; Rom. 1:20)?_____

_____

B. List some specific prophecies that look to Jesus as the Messiah and summarize their contents. _____

_____

C. What are qualities of the witnesses of Christ? _____

_____

D. What is the significance of "where" and "when" they first testified (Acts 2:1,22,32)? _____

_____

E. What do Scriptures claim for themselves (2 Tim. 3:16)?_____

_____

What facts about the Bible confirm this? _____

_____

III. Marriage Manual:

A. Who is in the best position to regulate family life and why (Gen. 1:26,27; 5:1; Eph. 4:6; Acts 17:24-29)?_____

_____

B. Who must men serve and why do they fail (Matt. 4:4,10; 7:21-28; Lk. 9:23; 1 John 2:15-17)?_____

_____

Conclusion:

A. Enumerate and discuss other relationships that test man's allegiance to God (Rom. 13:1,2; Eph. 6:5-9; Matt. 5:38-48)._____

_____

B. Who has all authority and what relationship do disciples sustain to that authority (Matt. 28:18; 10:24; John 8:31; Lk. 10:16)?_____

_____

Atmosphere of Love

Introduction

Family life, as life in general, can only survive in a suitable atmosphere. The climate of many homes gets a little stuffy on occasions and at times a little chilly. When the temperature drops rapidly and dips too low, a deep freeze sets in and the family suffers significant harm. Similar damage results if the temperature rises suddenly to the boiling point. The household is best served when a warm friendly spirit flows gently and evenly among the members of the family.

Families often differ over what produces this kind of environment. Households, however, that are headed by Christians have no doubts. They are given no multiple choice alternatives. Disciples under Christ, their Master, are controlled by the divine directives. These leaders know to set the thermostat on love and are assured by the divine will that the atmosphere will be perfectly regulated. Jesus unhesitantly stated the priority of love for his disciples when asked what is the greatest commandment.

The Priority of Love

Thou shalt love the Lord thy God with all thy heart, and with all thy soul, and with all thy mind. This is the great and first commandment. And a second like unto it is this, Thou shalt love thy neighbor as thyself. On these two commandments the whole law hangeth, and the prophets (Matt. 22:37-40)

Love, however, means different things to different people. Some view it as an electrifying emotional chemistry that sends pulsating charges from one person's feelings to another's. Others think of it as a free spirit of giving that accepts no restraints and is controlled by no rules. Although love may involve emotions and includes a spirit of giving, it is much more and is defined and described in unmistakable terms by the apostle Paul.

Love, it must first be understood, is governed by rules and comprehends all of God's commandments. The apostle Paul wrote: *"Thou shalt not commit adultery,"* *"Thou shalt not kill,"* *"Thou shalt not steal,"* and *"Thou shalt not covet."* He then adds: *"If there be any other commandment, it is summed up in this word, namely, Thou shalt love thy neighbor as thyself. Love worketh no ill to his neighbor; love therefore is the fulfillment of the law"* (Rom. 13:9,10).

When love prevails in the home, family members fulfill God's law by keeping his commandments. Loving husbands work no ill against their wives and loving wives work no ill against their husbands. So it is of fathers toward mothers, mothers toward fathers, parents toward children, and children toward parents and one another.

Love is more fully described by the same apostle in that grand chapter on love — 1 Corinthians 13. Paul speaks once again in specific and clear terms. He lists qualities of love that create an environment that adapts so suitably to the needs of family life. In other lessons space will be devoted to dictionary definitions of love, but before that families must learn and master the biblical description of love. Those features are detailed for Christians in the following passage:

> Love suffereth long, and is kind; love envieth not; love vaunteth not itself, is not puffed up, doth not behave itself unseemly, seeketh not its own, is not provoked, taketh not account of evil; rejoiceth not in unrighteousness, but rejoiceth with the truth; beareth all things, believeth all things, hopeth all things, endureth all things (1 Cor. 13:4-7).

Before enumerating these qualities, Paul underlined the necessity of love. Christians, he said, may give all their possessions to feed the poor or deliver their bodies to be burned as martyrs, but if they lack love they are nothing. They might, as was possible in the first century, speak in tongues, prophesy, or move mountains by faith and still be zero in God's eyes if love is missing (see 1 Cor. 13:1-3). Love is absolute. It is a must for Christians. An analysis of Paul's description of love will manifest its importance in the home. Until these facts are understood and accepted there is little point in considering further the biblical perspective of family life.

The Qualities of Love

1. Love Suffereth Long, Is Not Provoked. Two of the qualities of love relate to the control of passions. *"Suffereth long"* is frequently translated "patience." The Greek word is *makro,* meaning "long" or "large," and *thumos,* meaning "passion." It suggests the idea of "long passioned" or "long tempered," a contrast to the English expression "short tempered." The phrase *"is not provoked"* in some versions and commentaries is rendered "irritable." The word denotes the sharp stirring of man's spirit, a provocation of the soul, as Paul felt when he saw the abundance of idolatry in Athens (see Acts 17:16). The context of 1 Corinthians 13 implies, as the NIV translates it, that love is "not easily angered." Love controls the passions and keeps a cool head.

How vital this is to family life! When love exists husbands and wives are patient as they struggle through sexual adjustments, money-management problems, acceptance of one another's personal habits, and a host of tense circumstances. Husbands are not soon angry with their wives when there are no clean socks in the drawer or tuna salad sandwiches are served for supper. Wives do not rage against their husbands because the fence was not repaired yesterday or the sink is clogged and he's calmly watching Monday night football.

These principles equally apply to the difficulties of child training and discipline and to the tensions that develop between brothers and sisters. Love is patient and calm, qualities that seek explanations and search for understanding. Love eliminates short fuses that create an explosive atmosphere in the home.

2. Love is Kind. The New Testament word for "kind" comes from a family of words that means "useful" or "needful." The English word "kind" implies a charitable spirit and is generally used of deeds that supply some need. A cup of cold water for a thirsty man, a warm meal for a hungry person, or a coat for a destitute child are all seen as acts of kindness. Love is considerate and always provides what is of value or worth to the object of love. The kindness of God, for example, subjected Jesus to suffering and death because it was good for mankind (see Tit. 3:4,5). Kindness is always useful, even when sacrifice is demanded.

Kindness in the home determines what is worthwhile — be it chastisement of disobedient children, a spiritual lesson about obeying God, a helpful hand when important tasks become a burden, or a severe warning or scolding about hot stoves or dangerous streets. Love is compassionate and seeks to be useful in meeting the total needs of the family.

3. Love Envieth Not. The word for "envieth" in this verse is "jealous." The term originally meant to "boil with heat" and can refer to fiery zeal and enthusiasm for righteousness. Paul uses it here of the carnal spirit that often heats up between rivals. The apostle wrote earlier in this epistle about the competing parties in the church of Corinth and the jealousy that created division and strife. Warring factions arose because love for the well-being of one another and the church was absent (see 1 Cor. 3:1-4).

The same spirit often invades the home. Jealousy, as in the church, enters homes where the security of love is not present. Husbands, for example, who fail to assure their wives of their love can expect jealousy. They must likewise emphasize to their mates that as housewives they are valuable members of the family. Wives who are wrapped in the security of their husbands' love and praise are not threatened by the husbands' talk of what Mary or Sue has accomplished at the office.

This same assurance must envelope husbands when wives speak of Bill or Jim's good looks or expertise around the house. Parents likewise must carefully clothe their children with love and praise. Each child in his own right must know that he is loved and that he has value. Children are different in personalities and in talents and each must be esteemed for who he is. When each is secure in his own individuality, he will feel no rivalry or jealousy toward Johnny or Janey. Love envieth not and Christians who develop it and manifest it in the home will eliminate competition and jealousy.

4. Love Vaunteth Not, Is Not Puffed Up, Seeketh Not Its Own. Love, these qualities suggest, is not self-centered. The word "vaunteth" means in the noun form "a braggart." "Puffed up" refers to one who is inflated or swells up with his own importance; one who is proud or arrogant. A person who seeks his own puts himself at the center of life and demands that others gravitate toward him and orbit around his interest. Love, the apostle says, is not like that.

One of the basics of Christianity, Jesus taught, is *"he that humbleth himself shall be exalted"* (Lk. 14:11). Jesus also taught that the genuine expression of humility is service (Matt. 23:11,12), and that those who serve are greatest in the kingdom. So when Paul wrote to the church at Philippi, at a time when relationships were strained, he reminded them that Christians must each count one another better than themselves and they must each look to the things of others. This, he said, is the mind of Christ who humbled himself to serve mankind by death on the cross (see Phil. 2:1-9; Matt. 20:25-28).

Self — The Enemy Of Love

In marriage, there is an enemy of love far greater than hate. That enemy is *self*. It stands as a roadblock to all these expressions of love when we allow the "what's-in-it-for-me?" attitude, or just plain laziness, to dominate our personal lives.

Which points us to one of the most important keys to mutual fulfillment in marriage: *giving*. Considering . . . basic needs more important than our selfish desires. And the spirit of continual giving — of our time, our selves, our understanding — requires an unabashed brand of love (p. 140).

— Dan Benson, *The Total Man*

Husbands, as a later chapter will show, must love their wives as their own bodies. Proud, arrogant, self-centered husbands cannot possibly treat their wives with the same regard they have for themselves. When this spirit dominates the home, either in the husband or the wife, mates will be neglected, ignored and mistreated. Wives must esteem and respect their husbands, parents are to love their children, and children are to honor and obey their parents. Genuine humility and service in the home create an important climate in which every family member gives top priority to the others.

5. Love Does Not Behave Itself Unseemly. Some versions render this phrase, "Love . . . is not rude." Commentators often define it as "courtesy." "Unseemly" is translated from a word that can mean "shame" and describes conduct that is unsuitable for a Christian. It literally means "against the scheme," and denotes action that does not comport with God's scheme or plan for man. It might, for example, refer to lewd, lascivious, or immoral behavior (Rom. 13:13,14). On the other hand, it could describe a fit of anger, unfair treatment, curt snappy speech, or cold silent indifference.

Christians seek to grow into the maturity and perfection of Christ himself, including an understanding and practice of proper treatment of all family members. When Christians know how they ought to act, they avoid conduct toward one another that is shameful. Each family member knows his role and behaves appropriately toward all others. This eliminates many sources of tension and dissension. Love always acts properly.

6. Love Taketh Not Account Of Evil. This is another way of saying that love is forgiving. Paul uses a bookkeeping term that means to record or to put to the account of another. Love, he says, does not keep a record of evil. The term is also used to refer to the forgiveness Christians receive through faith. *"Blessed is the man to whom the Lord will not reckon sin"* (Rom. 4:8). In Christ by obedient faith God removes man's sins from the record book.

Christians easily forget the forgiveness they enjoy in Christ and remember the wrongs done against them by brethren (Eph. 4:31,32). They often carry around in their minds an imaginary black book in which they record all the misdeeds wrought against them and, at the slightest provocation, remind erring brothers. Love finds no place for grudges, but in the spirit of Christ forgives and forgets.

The importance of this in family life is obvious. Husbands and wives who at times get hysterical with one another, also, as one jokester put it, get "historical," a reference to bringing up the past. This creates an environment in which peace is suffocated in the heat of charge and counter charge. Storing up evil in one's heart to regurgitate at strategic moments is nothing more than spiritual and mental vomit that is unpleasant to behold and live with. Love keeps no record of past wrongs; it deals only with the present. Parents must likewise train their children to take no account of evil.

Love, in other words, as Paul further describes it, *"rejoices not in unrighteousness, but rejoiceth in truth."* A Christian who with joy points out the offenses of other family members is perverted in spirit. The recounting of bygone injustices is painful to the heart of one who loves good and hates evil. Truth bonds spirits together by forgiveness, whether in the church or the family.

7. Love Bears, Believes, Hopes and Endures All Things. The apostle completes his description of love by reminding Christians that love overcomes all obstacles. It bears up when problems are severe, trusts when confidence to others seems foolish, sees light when darkness hovers above, and remains firm under circumstances that would shake the feeble.

The Source Of Love

How beautiful heaven must be and how beautiful family life can be. The price, of course, is high. The Lord sets before Christians the strict standard of love. And surely none can doubt that by these qualities an ideal atmosphere for family life is created. How, though, can any family attain such goals? While none will reach the measure of perfection, an enabling power is available to strengthen God's people unto these results. It is too readily assumed that, since all men are human and make mistakes, the standard of love is impossible. Lack of perfection does not preclude the presence of love in the home of Christians.

Christians know, to begin with, that love is a fruit of the Spirit (Gal. 5:22,23). They know, secondly, that the Spirit strengthens the inward man with power. They know, thirdly, that when Christ dwells in their hearts by faith they are rooted and grounded in love. They know, finally, that faith comes by hearing and hearing comes by God's word. To assess this more fully, God's people must understand how the Spirit functions in their lives by the gospel (see Eph. 3:14-19; Rom. 10:17).

The Holy Spirit was promised by Jesus to the apostles that he might *"teach them all things"* and *"guide them into all truth."* The apostles were further taught that when the Spirit came upon them they would receive power and that they were to wait for that coming power at Jersualem. The Holy Spirit came to them at Jerusalem and they began to speak as the Spirit gave them utterance. The Spirit revealed unto them the mind of God, the mystery of the gospel held in secret from times eternal (see Jn. 14:25,26; 16:13; Acts 1:8; 2:1-4; 1 Cor. 2:6-13).

The gospel revealed by the Spirit is called the *"power of God."* It contains not only the scheme of redemption, but also the ability to build up and strengthen men unto the measure of the stature of Christ. The Greek word for "power" is the origin of our English word "dynamite," and describes a force from God that will enable a man to bear spiritual fruit. Jesus described it as a seed that enters "honest" and "good" hearts and produces fruit — some 30, some 60 and some 100 fold. This is the fruit of the Spirit Paul details to the Galatians, including love (see Rom. 1:16; Acts 20:32; Eph. 4:11-16; Lk. 8:11-15).

The gospel is also described as food: milk for the babes and meat for the fullgrown man in Christ. The word of God, as food for the body, must be assimilated into the soul of man to nourish and energize the spirit (see 1 Pet. 2:1,2; Heb. 5:11-14). Paul spoke of Timothy being *"nourished in the words of the faith, and of the good doctrine"* and to the Thessalonians of *"the word of God, which also worketh in you that believe"* (1 Tim. 4:6; 1 Thess. 2:13). The Greek word for "worketh" is the basis for the English word "energy," and alludes to the power that the nourishment of God's word provides for his people.

Conclusion

It is not enough for families to believe that God is, that Jesus is his Son, and that the Bible is inspired of God. It is not sufficient for families to intellectually reject humanism and to deplore its effect on this country. Families must turn off the TV, sit down with the Bible at hand, pray together, and take the time to ingest into their minds and persons the principles of righteousness. When truth pervades the entire beings of family members — love, peace, and joy will rule the home once again.

An Outline Study Guide

Introduction:
A. List and discuss specific attitudes that disrupt the home (Expand on the text).

_____

B. What general atmosphere best serves the interest of the home and what specific quality assures that?_____

_____

I. Priority of Love:
  A. What are the two greatest commands (Matt. 22:37-40)?_____

  _____

  B. What must control love (Jn. 14:15; Rom. 13:9,10)?_____

  _____

  List some examples_____
  C. Illustrate the necessity of love (1 Cor. 13:1-3)._____

  _____

II. Qualities of Love:
  A. Define "suffereth long" and "is not provoked."_____

  _____

  B. What is the primary meaning of "kindness"?_____

  _____

  C. "Envy" in 1 Corinthians 13 really means what?_____

  _____

How did it affect Corinth (1 Cor. 3:1-4)?_____

_____

How can it best be eliminated in the home?_____

_____

D. What expressions in 1 Corinthians 13 condemn pride? _____

_____

How should Christians view others (Phil. 2:3,4)?_____

_____

E. Define "unseemly"? _____

How might it have application in home life?_____

_____

F. Describe the origin of "taketh not account of evil."_____

_____

How does it relate to redemption (Rom. 4:8)?_____

_____

Why is it necessary in the home (Eph. 4:31,32)?_____

_____

III. Source of Love:
A. How is love produced (Gal. 5:22,23)?_____

What is the origin of strength in the inward man (Eph. 3:14-19)?_____

_____

How does faith come (Rom. 10:17)?_____

B. What is the work of the Spirit (John 14:25,26; 16:13)?_____

_____

How does the power of the gospel fill man (Rom. 1:16; Acts 20:32; Lk. 8:11-15)? _____

C. How are men nourished (1 Pet. 2:1,2; Heb. 5:11-14; 1 Tim. 4:6)?_____

Conclusion:
A. What must families believe and what must they reject as a basis for producing love?

_____

_____

B. What must homes do if love is to be assimilated into family members?___

_____

Design of Marriage

Introduction

Marriage, according to modern society, may be anything a couple wants it to be. It may be *temporary* — lasting till one of them meets someone they like more; *independent* — both following a career and passing one another like ships in the night; *open* — each free to date others and seek sexual fulfillment in extramarital affairs; *matriarchal* — agreeing for the wife and mother to rule the relationship; *homosexual* — accepting the right of mates to be of the same gender. That's right! That is what the world has come to. Anarchy in marriage reigns. Every man, as in the days of the judges (Judg. 21:25), does what is right in his own eyes.

Marriage to Christians, however, may only be what *God* designed it to be. God, they believe, created the human race, instituted marriage at the beginning, and has never altered his original plan. Jesus himself commended what the Father ordained. An overview of this sacred relationship as God planned it will orient Bible students for a specific and detailed analysis of the many aspects of marriage in subsequent lessons. What, then, according to God, is marriage?

Its Constituents

Marriage, to begin with, is the union of one male and one female. Jesus speaks of *"male"* and *"female"* and says *"the two shall become one flesh."* The beloved Son of God also says it was this way *"from the beginning"* (Matt. 19:4,5). In these few words the Lord addresses and combats many ancient and modern views of marriage. There is no excuse for misunderstanding God's original plan for marriage.

1. Monogamy. God, in the first place, never intended for marriage to degenerate into bigamy, polygamy, polyandry, polygyny, or any other relationship that includes more than one male and one female. Only the two — male and female — can be joined together by God. Neither economics, lust, benevolence, cultural bias, humanistic religion, nor other reasons must be permitted to distort the wisdom and beauty of God's creative will for the *"one flesh"* relationship of a man and a woman.

2. Heterosexual. God, moreover, did not authorize homosexual marriages, as a small segment of society now advocates. The Creator, in both Old Testament and New Testament, condemns the fleshly union of males with males and females with females. Jehovah dramatically — with destructive fire from heaven at Sodom and Gomorrah — revealed his hatred for homosexuality. He also says it is *"wicked"* and a *"very grievous"* sin (see Gen. 18,19). The apostle Paul called it a *"vile passion"* that is *"against nature"* and is *"worthy of death"* (Rom. 1:26,27,32).

3. Homo sapiens. God, finally, knowing the depths to which perverted men will sink, forbade the joining of humans with beasts. No beast, Jehovah determined at creation, is compatible or suitable for man's needs (Gen. 2:19,20). He, as a result, created woman to fulfill that role. Later, in his law to Moses, God specifically legislated against a man or woman uniting physically with a beast (see Lev. 20:15,16; Deut. 27:21).

Its Commitments

What is often called the "marriage law" is also stated by God at the beginning. *"Therefore,"* he says, *"shall a man leave his father and his mother, and shall cleave unto his wife: and they shall be one flesh"* (Gen. 2:24). Jesus spoke favorably of this "law" when he discussed marriage and divorce with the Pharisees (Matt. 19:5). A triangle is frequently used to diagram three commitments that God's order entails. Others prefer to view marriage as a three-legged stool that will collapse if any of the pledges go unfulfilled.

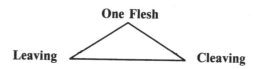

One Flesh

Leaving   **Cleaving**

1. Leave. Male and female who plan to marry must, first, commit themselves to *"leave"* father and mother. One gospel preacher was astounded by the reply of a divorce judge who said the number one cause of divorce in his court is *"in-laws"*! Marvel not, then, that Jesus used the intensive form of the word "leave" when he spoke of this pledge. The term means to forsake completely, "to abandon." This in no way annuls the command to honor one's father and mother, but underscores the need for children to renounce totally the rule of their parents over their households. A clear and final break must be made between a new family and the two original families. Fathers and mothers must not be permitted to interfere, regulate, dominate, or control the marriages of their children.

The Necessity Of Leaving

There can be no marriage without leaving. . . . This certainly is not something joyful. Where I come from tears are often shed when a wedding takes place. . . . Leaving is the price of happiness. There must be a clean and clear cut. Just as a newborn baby cannot grow up unless the umbilical cord is cut, just so marriage cannot grow up and develop so long as no real leaving, no clear separation from one's family, takes place. I say, this is hard. It is hard for the children to leave their parents. But it is just as hard for the parents to let their children go. . . . If no real leaving takes place, the marriage will be in trouble. . . . If you ask a Western marriage counselor [in contrast to African] which problem he has most frequently to deal with, he will probably answer, "With the mother-in-law problem" (pp. 13,14).

— **Walter Trobisch**, *I Married You*

---

2. Cleave. Secondly, a man and a woman must vow to *"cleave"* to one another. Marriage is not a tentative agreement. The Greek word used by Jesus *(kollao)* means "to glue or weld together" *(Harper's Analytical Lexicon)*. "To stick together like glue'' emphasizes the permanency of marriage. As Christians must *"cleave unto the Lord"* (Acts 11:23) *"unto death"* (Rev. 2:10), so husbands and wives must commit themselves "unto death do us part" (see Rom. 7:1,2; 1 Cor. 7:39). This pledge must be without reservation and must transcend all problems.

Often newlyweds hold divorce as an option available to them. "If it doesn't work out, we can always get a divorce" is an attitude that dooms the marriage before the glue gets dry. An escape hatch crafted into the marriage permits minor and insignificant problems to loom as perilous waters through which the relationship cannot be charted. Only when couples know that all conflicts must be settled do they have the will to weather each storm into calmer waters. The calm, it turns out, can be just as sure as the storm when the commitment to *"cleave unto"* one another and the maturity to face differences are present.

Handling Disagreements

The interesting fact is that one scientific analysis of 100 "successful" marriages and 200 "problem" marriages showed that people with happy marriages argue about the same things as people with unhappy marriages. The difference lies in how the couples handle their disagreements (p. 76).

— **Family Weekly** *via The Challenge of Being a Wife*

---

3. One Flesh. Man and woman, in the third place, consummate their commitments to one another when they unite themselves as *"one flesh."* The *"one flesh,"* according to a comment by the apostle Paul (1 Cor. 6:16), refers to sexual union of two bodies. Here Paul discusses an immoral oneness with a harlot, but the writer of Hebrews says the *"one flesh"* relationship in marriage is honorable and the bed is undefiled (Heb. 13:4). God created man and woman with physical and emotional desires for one another and demands a commitment by each to fulfill the sexual needs of the other (see 1 Cor. 7:1-6). The uniting of the bodies of a husband and wife as *"one flesh"* is a fitting expression of the intimacy, boundless sharing, and total merging that marriage demands of a male and female.

4. Civil Law. God demands that his people comply with all laws enacted by civil powers (Rom. 13:1,2; 1 Pet. 2:13-17). This, of course, includes marriage laws. Trobisch says "so long as they are not ready to take the legal step, they are not ready to take full responsibility for each other. Responsibility calls for legality" *(I Married You,* p. 80). Although legality must not be minimized, marriage is essentially complete when one male and one female commit themselves to leave father and mother, cleave to one another, and unite as one flesh.

Its Companionship

God knew at creation that man without a companion was incomplete. *"And Jehovah said, It is not good that the man should be alone; I will make a help meet for him"* (Gen. 2:18). The loneliness of man without woman highlights another important feature of marriage. The creation of woman and the design of marriage reveal the demands for companionship in the husband-wife relationship. When God saw man was alone, he took one of his ribs and *"from the man made he a woman and brought her unto the man"* (Gen. 2:22).

Woman Answers Man's Needs

After examining all other creatures, God found none of them suitable for man, so he made a special creature that surpasses all other creatures on earth in beauty, charm, tenderness, and virtue. When a woman recognizes these qualities are her superior ones, she tends to provide what her husband needs. No activity is higher for a woman than being a good wife and homemaker. Any direction she may go from that high position is down (pp. 20,21).

— **Roland Lewis** *via The Challenge of Being a Wife*

Woman is bone of man's bones and flesh of man's flesh and stands by his side in marriage to dispel the desolate emptiness that rules his spirit without her. She is there as a friend, as his helper, as a companion to fill a gaping void in his being. A vital part of marriage is social interplay between a husband and a wife. Those who have lost mates by death will affirm that absence of companionship is their greatest loss. Husbands and wives as friends to discuss events of the day, to interact in resolving problems, to share laughs or tears — fills one of the most basic needs of the human race. Successful marriages provide this.

"Hollywood marriages" have made a farce of this design in marriage. Husbands and wives cannot be companions to one another when one of them is at one location for weeks or months making a movie and the other is half-way around the world on a different set. Absence from one another starves friendship and the social bond that cements the two emotionally. Inner malnutrition sets in when intimate association is lacking. Marital death results. The divorce rate among the "stars" demonstrates the value of companionship to the life of a marriage.

Its Relationship

The terms *"husband"* and *"wife"* denote the relationship between a male and female in marriage. The two have different roles. The husband is to be a loving head and the wife is to be a submissive helper. Because man was first formed and then woman and because woman was deceived when they both sinned at the beginning, God assigned man the rule over the relationship and woman the role of subjection (see Gen. 3:16; 1 Cor. 11:3,8-10; 1 Tim. 2:11-14).

The feminist movement has influenced much of modern society to reject these roles in marriage. That rejection stems, however, from abuses of the roles and misunderstanding of what God actually teaches about husbands and wives.

First, God did not declare the superiority of man and the inferiority of woman. The roles of each have nothing to do with intellectual capacities and make no statement concerning equality or inequality. Second, the unloving and dictatorial rule of some husbands in marriage is a perversion of what God designed and what the Scriptures authorize. When the responsibilities of husband and wife are understood and performed, the relationship is beautiful and pleasant for both. The women's movement is not fighting God's will so much as it is reacting against modern distortions of that will.

1. Husbands. Husbands, for example, are to love their wives *"even as Christ loved the church, and gave himself for it";* they are *"to love their own wives as their own* *bodies"* (Eph. 5:25,28). The husband who has the love of Christ will, in his rule, place the needs of his wife above his own. Loving leadership by husbands will eliminate the animosity toward men that now reigns among many of today's women. When husbands manifest the beauty of sacrificial love toward their wives, women will find submission much more palatable. This kind of rule is the missing ingredient that has left a bad taste in the mouths of modern women toward men and marriage.

True Leadership

Leadership is committed to promoting the best interests of those who are led. There is no room for selfishness in true leadership. *It is the farthest thing from dictatorship.* A dictator is interested only in *his* goals and *at the center of his goals is himself.* He may do many good things for others, but behind all he does are his own interests. . . True leadership cannot be divorced from true love. They are part of each other. A leader in this sense *is prepared to sacrifice himself for the sake of those he leads* (p. 81).

— **Fred Renich,** *The Christian Husband*

---

2. Wives. Wives, when husbands faithfully fulfill their roles, will have little difficulty including "obey" in their marriage vows. They will readily submit themselves in "reverence" — respect and esteem — to their own husbands (Eph. 5:22-24, 33). They would not even balk at calling their husbands "lord," as Sarah did Abraham (1 Pet. 3:6). They might even find time and the will to dust off his throne and meet his needs for a homemaker and housewife. Detailed analysis of this relationship must be reserved for later lessons.

The Woman of Proverbs 31

The worthy woman portrayed in this passage holds an honored position, has influence over many, and receives deserved praise. Today women are bombarded by the belief that the position of wife and mother is without honor, that her influence is limited, and that she is "just a housewife." This is not the true picture of the worthy woman of Proverbs 31, and it is not true of the modern homemaker. . . . When a woman feels her worth and the value of her position as homemaker, she is a willing worker who is able to set in motion her household system and keep it running smoothly, knowing its importance to herself and others (Introduction, p. 91).

— **Darlene Craig,** *A Worthy Woman*

Its Permanency

A few additional thoughts must be expressed about the permanency of marriage. Marriage, as husbands and wives vow, is "for as long as you both shall live." The apostle Paul said, *"The woman that hath a husband is bound by the law to the husband while he liveth"* (Rom. 7:2; 1 Cor. 7:39). When Pharisees came to Jesus about divorce, they asked whether a man could put away his wife for *"every cause."* Jesus said three things.

Jesus, first, quoted the original marriage law that a man must *"cleave to his wife."* This means, as already noted, that a man and woman are "welded" together in marriage. A permanent bond is secured by their commitment to stick together like glue. Next Jesus added: *"What therefore God hath joined together, let not man put asunder."* When the Pharisees then argued that Moses granted divorces for every cause, Jesus replied — *"from the beginning it hath not been so"* (Matt. 19:1-8).

Jesus, in a final remark, gave one exception for divorce. *"And I say unto you, Whosoever shall put away his wife, except for fornication, and shall marry another, committeth adultery: and he that marrieth her when she is put away committeth adultery"* (Matt. 19:9; see also Matt. 5:31,32). A mate, Jesus says, who commits adultery violates the sacred purity of the *"one flesh"* relationship and frees the innocent partner to divorce him and remarry. Scripture grants no other reason to sever what God in marriage has permanently joined and bound together.

Conclusion
The goal in subsequent lessons is to elaborate on these principles and others that relate to family life. Marriage was designed by God for the happiness of man and woman. It is only by his plan that the needs of each other are fully satisfied and the fullness of joy is realized.

Later chapters will specifically detail the husband's relationship to his wife, the wife's role as helper to the husband, the father and mother's responsibilities to their children, the children's obligation to honor and obey their parents, the problems of "working" and "parenting," the issue of divorce and remarriage, and the basis for choosing a husband or wife.

Effort will always be made to understand marriage and family life as God designed it. The writer has no interest at all in the wisdom of man and in adding to the anarchy that already rules modern views of marriage. To know the teaching of the Creator — who is all wise and all caring — is the one goal of these studies.

An Outline Study Guide
Introduction:
A. List and discuss some modern views of marriage._____

_____

B. How would the period of the Judges characterize these views (Judg. 21:25)?

_____

I. Constituents:
A. How many and who did marriage originally include (Matt. 19:4,5)?___

_____

B. What is meant by monogamy?_____

Bigamy? _____

Polygamy? _____

Polyandry? _____

Polygyny?_____

C. What does "heterosexual" mean?_____

How does God feel about "homosexuality" (Gen. 18:20,23; 19:7,24,25; Rom. 1:26,27,32)? _____

_____

D. Why would God discuss "beast-man" relationships?_____

_____

What does he say about them (Lev. 20:15,16; Deut. 27:21)?_____

_____

II. Commitments:
A. State the original marriage law (Gen. 2:24)._____

_____

B. Define the word "leave" used by Jesus._____

In what sense is abandonment not meant (Mk. 7:10-13; 1 Tim. 5:4)?____

_____

In what sense is it necessary?_____

C. What does "cleave" literally mean?_____

How long should a marriage last (Rom. 7:1,2; 1 Cor. 7:39)?_____

_____

D. To what does "one flesh" refer (1 Cor. 6:16)?_____

What is said about the purity of this relationship in marriage (Heb. 13:4)?

_____

E. In what way does civil law relate to marriage (Rom. 13:1,2; 1 Pet. 2:13,17)?

_____

III. Companionship:
A. What did God say about man before he made woman (Gen. 2:18)?____

_____

B. To what important function in marriage does this point?_____

_____

How do "Hollywood marriages" illustrate the importance of companionship?

_____

C. List and discuss ways husbands and wives can be companions?_____

_____

IV. Relationship:
A. Why did God assign husbands the rule (Gen. 3:16; 1 Cor. 11:8-10; 1 Tim. 2:11-14)? _____

_____

B. State how husbands are to rule their wives (Eph. 5:25,28,29)._____

_____

C. What attitude are wives to have (Eph. 5:22-24,33)?_____

_____

What did Sarah call Abraham (1 Pet. 3:6)?_____

V. Permanency:
A. What does Jesus say about permanency of marriage (Matt. 19:6)?_____

_____

B. What exception does Jesus give for divorce and remarriage (Matt. 19:9; 5:31, 32)? _____

_____

Conclusion:
A. What is the only way to happiness in marriage?_____

_____

B. What is the goal of this study?_____

_____

Love Your Wives

Introduction

Marital death is rampant in this so-called "Christian" nation. No one needs a Gallup or Harris poll to detect that. Look next door, across the street, or around the corner to see the lifeless remains of shattered unions that once breathed the breath of married life. Observe relatives — grandparents, parents, brothers, sisters, uncles, aunts — who have put asunder what God joined together. Count the preachers, elders, deacons, and other Christians who have gone back on their vow — "unto death do us part." Statistics are unnecessary to confirm the epidemic that threatens family life in this country.

That husband-wife relationships lack something vital to their health and well-being may be the understatement of the century. Surveys, questionnaires, clinics, and studies galore have dissected marriage corpses in an effort to find fatal anatomical flaws. Hundreds of books based on these autopsy reports have cited numerous causes for marital death and all of them, no doubt, are important factors. The one factor, however, that must head the list is the failure of husbands to love their wives as Christ loved the church. The day the vaccine of "husband love" is injected into dying marriages that day the tide of the epidemic will be rolled back.

Love As Christ

The problem of wholesome relationships is complicated by our native self-centeredness. Even a man's love for his wife is distorted by selfishness, so that his innate ideas about love focus on what he is to *get* from loving rather than what he can *give* to his wife as her lover. The answer to the seemingly hopeless barrier to husband-wife oneness has been demonstrated by Christ himself. The key is found, for husbands, in the command: "Husbands, love your wives *as Christ also loved the church*" (p. 239).

— **Fred Renich,** *The Christian Husband*

The breakdown of any relationship, be it business, political, or marital, can usually be traced to its leadership. The husband is the *"head of the wife"* and, as the ruler of the marriage, must bear chief responsibility for its failure. Where husbands have failed, more often than not, is to love their wives as Christ loved the church and to give themselves for their wives as Christ gave himself for the church. Sacrificial love, as this lesson will show, is the basis for the husband's rule of his wife and is the spirit that will breathe life into any marriage. The husband's duty to love his wife is stated plainly by the apostle Paul:

Husbands, love your wives, even as Christ also loved the church, and gave himself for it. . . . Even so ought husbands also to love their own wives as their own bodies . . . for no man ever hated his own flesh; but nourisheth and cherisheth it, even as Christ also the church (Eph. 5:25,28,29).

The Word Love

The English word "love" covers a multitude of feelings, desires, concerns, and translates a variety of terms used by ancient Greeks. The same word is used in English to describe a man's taste for strawberries that is used to describe his affection for his wife. But does "I love strawberries" mean the same thing as "I love my wife"? Fortunately, Greek, the language of the New Testament, had more than one word to denote what is commonly called "love." To understand three of those words is to narrow down the meaning of Paul's instruction to husbands. To grasp and practice what Paul commands husbands is to discover power that will give life and strength to the feeblest of marriages.

1. *Eros,* Lust. Paul does not use *eros* or *erao,* the Greek words for physical or sexual love. These words are equivalent to "fleshly lust" and denote the sensual desire a man feels for a woman. The English word "erotic," meaning "to arouse sexual desire," originates here. *Eros* or lust is a legitimate desire of a husband for his wife (see 1 Cor. 7:1-7), but falls far short of the love Paul commands and the love that builds successful marriages.

2. *Philos,* Feeling. Neither does the apostle use the words *philos* or *phileo,* terms that describe friendship, affection, feelings, or emotional attachment. A warmth and glow are inherent in these words that are important to marriage. Husbands and wives are to be best friends and devoted companions to one another, but this too is beneath the love that Christ had for the church and the love that gives stability to marriage.

3. *Agape,* Devotion. *Agape* or *agapao,* the basis for Paul's instruction to husbands, means devotion, concern, good will, dedication, commitment — all those noble words that mean to care. It is not a love that is sensual or emotional, but intellectual — a love that has an interest in another's well-being. It is an active love that resolves or wills to provide. It is, therefore, a love that can be commanded as a duty.

Jesus said, for example, *"Love your enemies, and pray for them that persecute you"* (Matt. 5:44). Jesus does not command the feelings to be affectionate, but orders the will to care and actively devote itself to the needs of its foes. In addition to prayer, the physical needs of enemies are to be supplied (see Rom. 12:20,21). One can decide to do this as a matter of what is right. It depends not on emotional attachment, but on commitment to truth.

Giving Of Ourselves

We may or may not have that euphoric, ooey-gooey feelings that the world has termed "love." We may be good providers, good at giving gifts and taking her out to dinner, or good sex partners. But where we often hit a snag is in giving of *ourselves.* It's hard. It's contrary to our selfish human nature. But it's what our wives need most (p. 146).
— **Dan Benson,** *The Total Man*

This love is what William Barclay called "unconquerable benevolence" and "undefeatable good will." Since it is dedicated to what is right, it is not affected by the unloveliness of the one loved. *Agape* is benevolent and good even when it is undeserved. It cares and gives and sacrifices for the sake of principles. Christ in death personifies *agape* — the love husbands are commanded to give to their wives.

The Love of Christ

Jesus loved the world and gave himself for it. *"Hereby know we love, because he laid down his life for us"* (1 Jn. 3:16). Nothing anyone had done or might do could conquer the devotion of the Lord to man's salvation. Not even those who slapped him, mocked him, spit on him, and nailed him to the cross could destroy his love for them. Jesus died for them too, and in the final minutes of his life pleaded for them: *"Father, forgive them: for they know not what they do"* (Lk. 23:34). While men were weak in ungodliness and sin, Jesus died for them — for con-artists, child-molesters, wife-beaters, murderers, homosexuals, drunkards, thieves, etc. (Rom. 5:6-8).

1. Sacrificial. *Agape,* as seen in Christ's love, is, first of all, sacrificial. Paul says Jesus *"gave himself up"* for the church (Eph. 5:25). The Son of God came not to earth in the interest of himself. He counted not equality with God a thing to cling to and gave up all the prerogatives and rights of heaven (Phil. 2:5,6). *"Though he was rich, yet for your sakes he became poor, that ye through his poverty might become rich"* (2 Cor. 8:9).

A husband, therefore, who imitates Christ, will not in marriage put his own needs first. The wife must be number one. A husband must deny himself, set aside his own interests, and will what is good for the wife. And nothing his wife does or says must interfere with and defeat the unselfish spirit that promotes her well being. A marriages thrives on this kind of care.

2. Service. Sacrificial love also demands actions. Jesus not only emptied himself of heaven's wealth, but took on the *"form of a servant"* to meet the needs of sinners. To supply those needs he became *"obedient even unto death, yea, the death of the cross"* (Phil. 2:7,8). Jesus *"came not to be ministered to, but to minister, and to give his life a ransom for many"* (Matt. 20:28). Service after the example of Jesus makes men great in the kingdom (Matt. 20:25-27); it likewise makes men great in the family domain. *Agape* serves. So do husbands who possess it.

The Warm Cloak Of Love

Dr. Bovet compares the love of the husband to a warm cloak. As long as the wife feels encircled, wrapped up in this cloak, she is able to surrender herself completely and unconditionally to her husband, both body and mind. In order to give her this feeling of being sheltered, the husband has to learn that it is not unmanly to express his feelings. If his words and caresses go together with the attitude of his heart, they will convey to her the message, "I am loved" (p. 22).

— **Ingrid Trobishch**, *The Joy of Being a Woman*

Loving husbands look to the needs of their wives when they need an hour or two relief from the burden of children at the end of a grueling day. They take on the form of servants and offer a few words of praise and a back rub when their wives are struggling with an emotional downer at a certain time in their cycle. Husbands with *agape* push a vacuum sweeper or minister at a sink full of dirty dishes when extreme circumstances put their wives behind in the household chores. Wimpy? No! This, husbands, is the love of Christ. *Agape* demands it, marriages need it, and wives will submit to it. This is the stuff of husbanding!

The Love of Self

A husband's love for his wife is also compared to his love for himself. *"Even so ought husbands also to love their wives as their own bodies. He that loveth his own wife loveth himself: for no man ever hated his own flesh; but nourisheth and cherisheth it, even as Christ the church"* (Eph. 5:28,29). The care, Paul says, that a husband has for himself and his own needs becomes the basis for loving his wife.

This principle is as old as the law of Moses. There Jehovah said: *"Thou shalt not hate thy brother in thy heart: thou shalt surely rebuke thy neighbor, and not bear sin because of him. Thou shalt not take vengeance, nor bear any grudge against the children of thy people; but thou shalt love thy neighbor as thyself"* (Lev. 19:17,18). Jesus says this law is the second greatest command (Matt. 22:39). What this command means to Christians and husbands is what men often call the "Golden Rule." *"All things therefore whatsoever ye would that men should do unto you, even so do you also unto them: for this is the law and the prophets"* (Matt. 7:12).

Husbands who can see their wives' needs with the clarity they see their own needs have learned the secret of happy marriages. As good neighbors put themselves in their neighbors' shoes before they speak or act, so good husbands slip on their wives' sandals to see what love demands. This is called understanding and love without it is blind.

Elkanah's Understanding Of Hannah

When Hannah was sad and distraught because Peninnah ridiculed her for her barren womb, Elkanah was concerned by Hannah's tears and loss of appetite. He was aware of her emotional and physical needs. He was aware of her tears, her appetite, and her heart as he said, *"Hannah, why weepest thou? and why eatest thou not? and why is thy heart grieved?"* He was sensitive to her very heart. He then tugged at her heart with a question, *"Am I not better to thee than ten sons?"* His question showed they had communicated. He was conscious of her aching heart and now knew the reason for it (p. 18).

— **Darlene Craig**, *A Worthy Woman*

---

1. Nourishes Her. Husbands, who love their wives as themselves, *"nourisheth"* them, Paul says, *"even as Christ also the church."* The word "nourish" means to "promote health and strength" *(Harper's Analytical Lexicon)* and refers primarily to the upbringing and nurturing of children (see Eph. 6:4). The term incorporates the whole training of children — physically, mentally, emotionally, spiritually, socially. Husbands, the word implies, supply strength for the health of their wives' total being. Nothing may be neglected or ignored in securing the wholeness of their person.

2. Cherishes Her. Husbands likewise *"cherisheth"* their wives as their own flesh. The word "cherish" means literally to "impart warmth" and was used originally to denote birds that warm their young by gathering them under their wings. The idea is again reminiscent of Christ's love. *"How often,"* he said to the nation of Israel, *"would I have gathered thy children together, even as a hen gathereth her chickens under her wings, and ye would not"* (Matt. 23:37). Although they refused, Jesus gave himself unselfishly and untiringly to the spiritual needs of his own race. He really cared!

"Nourish" and "cherish" suggest the compassion and concern husbands must have for their wives. Scripture does not portray them as "macho" men who are too rough and too tough to literally gather their wives into their arms to caress and stroke them physically and emotionally unto good health. Men, more than women, need to be liberated — freed from an image that precludes tears, kind words, a gentle disposition and soft touch. Both their wives and their marriages need this.

Love Has No Boundaries

What is fundamental to husbands' rule of their wives is the quality of the husbands themselves. Ideal marriages rest on the spiritual development of husbands after the likeness of Christ. Until husbands by the power of the gospel bear in their lives the fruit of the Spirit (Gal. 5:22,23), they will not be transformed into the image of God's Son (Rom. 8:29) and will not translate that image into loving leadership in marriage. When Christ reigns in their hearts, husbands will set no boundaries around their love.

1. Unlimited Love. Husbands are not qualified to rule their wives lovingly until they have unlimited love. The love of Christ for the church drew no lines — not even at death. Nothing was too good for the church. When husbands set limits on what they will do for the welfare and joy of their wives, the foundation of marriage already shows cracks.

2. Unending Love. Husbands who rule well their wives love them unceasingly. There can be no compromise with the vow to love one's wife until death. If *"no man ever hateth his own flesh,"* as Paul wrote, then he can *never* cease to love his wife. The day husbands despise or are indifferent toward their wives is the day the soundness of the marriage begins to suffer. As Christ ever liveth to make intercession for the needs of the saints (Heb. 4:14-16; 7:23-25), so husbands ever live to provide for the needs of their wives.

3. Unselfish Love. The key to all of this, as already noted, is the unselfish love of husbands. What was written by the pen of the apostle Paul is the real story of husbands' relationship to their wives. No writer in history has exalted women to such heights and championed so fiercely their rights — their right to be loved, their right to be served, their right to be protected. Husbands who fence themselves in and shut out their wives deny them these rights and build barriers that hinder the bond of oneness so essential to the survival of marriage.

Conclusion

Paul's story of the role of husbands has been poorly told and grossly misinterpreted in the lives of selfish, inhuman, unloving husbands. This distorted account has captured the thinking of modern society, especially the feminist movement, and Paul is often portrayed as a "woman hater." Women today conclude that the Bible views wives as abused creatures, slaves — inferior nobodies who have nothing of value to offer the world. Had husbands loved their wives as Paul taught, wives would have felt loved, and honored, and appreciated. They would have recognized themselves as persons of worth, esteemed themselves as beings of inner beauty, and viewed themselves as queens of the home.

Modern wives, as a result, would, as God ordained, be content to love their husbands, submit to their rule, direct the households, and care for the children. What spiritual beauty has been sacrificed on the altar of selfishness, where husbands offered not themselves in the love of Christ but their wives in the love of themselves. Husbands must repent with sackcloth and ashes.

Husbands who repent are ready to move to the next lesson on *Head of the Wife.* Until husbands commit themselves to genuine love, they will abuse the rule of their households, deny honor to their wives as weaker vessels, and refuse to dwell with their mates according to knowledge — topics to be taken up next in a study of specific responsibilities of husbands.

An Outline Study Guide

Introduction:

A. List factors causing divorce._____

_____

What is the chief one this chapter deals with?_____

_____

B. What two examples of love are the basis for a man's love of his wife (Eph. 5:25, 28,29)? _____

_____

I. The Word Love:

A. *Eros:* What is its essential meaning?_____

_____

Why does it have a place in marriage (1 Cor. 7:1-6; Heb. 13:4)?_____

_____

B. *Philos:* What does this word describe?_____

_____

To what part of the mind does it relate?_____

_____

C. *Agape:* What are some synonyms for this word?_____

_____ , _____

To what part of the mind does it relate?_____

_____

What definition does William Barclay give it?_____

_____

D. In what sense can a person love his enemies (Matt. 5:38-47; Rom. 12:17-21)?

_____

II. Love of Christ:

A. How did Christ show his love for enemies (Lk. 23:34)?_____

_____

B. Describe what Christ gave up and what he became for man (Phil. 2:5,6; 2 Cor. 8:9)?_____

_____

List and discuss things husbands must give up for their wives._____

_____

C. Jesus served mankind by giving what (Phil. 2:7,8; Matt. 20:28)?_____

In what ways can husbands serve their wives?_____

_____

III. Love Of Self:

A. How does Paul describe a husband's love for himself (Eph. 5:28,29)?__

_____

How did Moses state this principle (Lev. 19:17,18)?_____

_____

How does the "Golden Rule" put it (Matt. 7:12)?_____

_____

B. *Nourishes.* Define "nourish."_____

_____

Based on its meaning in child rearing (Eph. 6:4) list areas of application in husbands' relationship to wives: _____, _____,

_____, _____.

C. *Cherishes.* What did this originally mean?_____

_____

How did Jesus apply it spiritually in his attitude toward Jews (Matt. 23:37)?

_____

What might this literally suggest to husbands?_____

_____

IV. Love Has No Boundaries:

A. What does it mean for a husband to set no limits on his love?_____

_____

How far can one take this?_____

B. What "phrase" indicates that man cannot cease to love his wife (Eph. 5:29)?

_____

What does Jesus "ever" do and provide for the saints that illustrates this point (Heb. 7:23-25; 4:14-15)?_____

_____

Conclusion:

A. Why, in part, do feminists feel as they do about men?_____

_____

B. How would women feel if properly loved by men?_____

_____

Head of the Wife

Introduction

The role of the husband as head of the wife is an occasion for much misunderstanding, fierce animosity, and outright rejection of God's design for the home. The shallow view that the husband merely stands atop the marriage relationship as a chief executive to make decisions and issue orders to the wife is both a distortion and abuse of God's plan. A husband who so sees his role will be as cold and calculating as the corporate president who views employees as unfeeling puppets he must control to satisfy his capitalistic greed.

Many husbands, no doubt, think of their wives as servants and rule them in the absence of love. And such husbands may be the rule rather than the exception. God, nonetheless, did not plan it this way and husbands of that persuasion are not spiritually prepared to be the heads of their wives. Men must eradicate from their minds the male chauvinist view of husbands portrayed in the once popular country song written by Shel Silverstein.

Put Another Log On The Fire

Put another log on the fire
Cook me up some bacon and some beans
And go out to the car and change the tire
Wash my socks and sew my old blue jeans

Come on, Baby

You can fill my pipe and then go fetch my slippers
And boil me up another pot of tea
Then put another log on the fire, Babe
And come and tell me why you're leavin' me.

Now, don't I let you wash the car on Sunday?
Don't I warn you when you're getting fat?
Ain't I gonna take you fishin' someday?
Well, a man can't love a woman more than that.

Ain't I always nice to your kid sister?
Don't I take her drivin' every night?
So, sit here at my feet
'Cause I like you when you're sweet
And you know it ain't feminine to fight.

Come on, Baby.

You can fill my pipe
And then go fetch my slippers
And then boil me up another pot of tea
Then put another log on the fire, Babe
And come and tell me why you're leavin' me.

Christ is the example for husbands to imitate and it is not the picture Silverstein paints. Hear the biblical instructions: *"For the husband is the head of the wife, as Christ also is the head of the church, being himself the savior of the body"* (Eph. 5:23).

Head of the Wife

The husband's rule of the wife, as his love for her, is illustrated by the rule of Christ over the church. What an exacting standard! And one not to be taken lightly by husbands. Husbands, as a prelude to ruling their wives, must commit themselves to understanding Christ's rule of the church. That rule, as will be seen, blends imperceptibly and flawlessly with love.

Christ is not only known as "head" of the church, but is called "master" or, in Greek, *despotes* (see 2 Tim. 2:21; 2 Pet. 2:1). *Despotes* is the origin of the English word "despot" and means dictator or absolute ruler. Husbands are likewise portrayed as "lord" of the marriage relationship, a term Sarah used to describe her husband Abraham (1 Pet. 3:6). As the head controls the body totally, so husbands as heads or lords of their wives rule absolutely. Sound harsh? Yes, until one understands how the despotic rule of Christ over the church proceeds so beautifully from his bosom of infinite love. Christ, politically speaking, is a "benevolent dictator." He rules in the interest of his subjects. So do loving husbands.

Jesus, for example, calls all men: *"Come unto me"* and *"take my yoke upon you"* (Matt 11:28,29). Although he has *"all authority"* and men must *"hearken in all things"* to him (Matt. 28:18; Acts 3:22,23), Christ beckons them and rules them for their own good. Those who enter the yoke with Christ shall, he says, *"find rest for your souls"* (Matt. 11:29). This is also spelled out in the beatitudes, the Lord's assurances of happiness to his subjects (Matt. 5:1-12). The word *"blessed,"* as William Barclay translates it, means "bliss" — the promised peace and joy the Lord offers his kingdom citizens.

Husbands who walk in the footsteps of Jesus will rule as benevolent lords. That husbands are to be the "head" (Eph. 5:23) of the wives and are to "rule" their households (1 Tim. 3:5) cannot be disputed. But what must be argued strenuously is a headship and rule that put the husband's interest before the needs of the wife. A husband who rules as Christ rules elevates the happiness of the wife to the place of chief concern. A Christ-like groom takes a bride because he loves her, seeks her good, wants to provide for her, and plans to satisfy her deepest needs.

Unselfish husbands approach marriage to *give* not to *get*. Men who try to build marriages on demand for power, lust for sex, or need for a servant are like foolish men who build houses on sand (see Matt. 7:24-27). Unless husbands are heads of their wives as Christ is head of his church, an enduring foundation for marriage has not been laid.

A husband, for example, who will not put his wife ahead of golf or bowling, nights out with the guys, relaxed evenings in the lazyboy, or time in a woodworking or hobby shop has no fellowship with the spirit of Christ and has not learned the meaning of "giving himself" to his wife. While these activities have a place, a wife must not be left to wonder about her husband's love and her place as number one in his heart.

Honor the Wife

The benevolent rule of a husband is reflected in the honor he gives to his wife. *"Ye husbands,"* Peter says, *"in like manner, dwell with your wives according to knowledge, giving honor unto the woman, as the weaker vessel"* (1 Pet. 3:7). The thought behind the word "honor" is "primarily a valuing, hence, objectively, a price paid" (Vine, *Expository Dictionary of New Testament Words).* As vessels of gold or silver in a great house are valued with honor and treated with singular care (2 Tim. 2:20), so wives are to be exalted as priceless companions. The Proverbs say: *"A worthy woman who can find? For her price is far above rubies. . . Whoso findeth a wife finded a good thing, and obtaineth a favor of Jehovah"* (Prov. 31:10; 18:22).

More valuable than the paycheck the husband brings home and of greater worth than all the jewels that bedeck her body is the wife herself. Her value raises serious questions for her husband. Is his esteem for her manifest in his decisions, in his actions, in his words? Does he express his appreciation to her? Is what she means to him made evident to her? Does he praise her? Does he extol her worth? Lemuel says of the worthy woman's husband: *"Her children rise up, and call her blessed; her husband also, and he praiseth her, saying, many daughters have done worthily, but thou excellest them all"* (Prov. 31:28).

"Tell Her So"

Amid the cares of married strife,
In spite of toil and business life,
If you value your sweet wife,
 Tell her so!

When days are dark and deeply blue
She has her troubles, same as you
Show her that your love is true —
 Tell her so!

There was a time you thought it bliss
To get the favor of one kiss;
A dozen now won't come amiss —
 Tell her so!

Don't act, if she has passed her prime
As tho' to please her were a crime;
If ever you loved her, now's the time —
 Tell her so!

She'll return, for each caress,
An hundredfold of tenderness!
Hearts like hers were made to bless!
 Tell her so!

You are hers and hers alone;

Well you know she's all your own;
Don't wait to carve it on a stone —
Tell her so!

Never let her heart grow cold —
Richer beauties will unfold;
She is worth her weight in gold!
Tell her so!

— Author Unknown

The wife of a loving husband occupies an exalted position in his heart. He respects her as a person made in God's image, protects and helps her as a weaker vessel, befriends her as a companion worthy of special care, and extols her as valuable helper in family life. He may then rule her, knowing that his leadership will bestow no undue burdens, neglect no unfulfilled needs, exercise no tyrannical disregard, and display no physical abuse. He will, in short, seek to understand her and provide for her.

Hear the Wife

Understanding! That is the first goal of every husband who rules his wife as Christ rules the church. Communication is essential to understanding and listening is necessary to communication. That parties in any relationship, including marriage, must listen to one another is basic. The failure of husbands to give ear to what their wives are trying to communicate is high on the list of factors contributing to the breakup of marriages today. Busy, tired, moody, self-centered, uncaring husbands hardly notice wives who are all but screaming for their attention. Wives for the most part are willing to talk and husbands for the most part are not listening. Husbands who look to Christ as the model for leadership in the home will take to heart Peter's charge: *"Ye husbands, in like manner, dwell with your wives according to knowledge"* (1 Pet. 3:7).

The exact scope of Peter's charge may be uncertain. He may refer to understanding God's word concerning life as a Christian, but dwelling with one's wife according to knowledge surely includes knowing *her*. A husband who loves and honors his wife seeks to know her thoroughly. Only then can he be a caring head who gives himself and his time to meet her needs.

1. Spiritual Needs. A caring husband, first of all, understands his wife's spiritual needs. As Joshua, he will learn God's will and decide what is good for their relationship to God. *"Choose you this day whom ye will serve,"* the ancient warrior challenged Israel, when contrasting Jehovah to idols. Then came his answer. *"But as for me and my house, we will serve Jehovah"* (Josh. 24:15). A faithful husband today, as Stephanas (1 Cor. 16:15), will direct his family in service to God. He will lead them in Bible study, in prayer, in assembling with the saints, in character, and other spiritual activities.

2. Physical Needs. A caring husband will likewise understand his wife's physical needs. He knows, to begin with, her need for material necessities. Man was charged from the first to provide *"bread"* by *"the sweat of his face"* for the woman (Gen. 3:19). A man who will not provide for his family is, according to Paul, worse than an infidel (1 Tim. 5:8). A husband who, out of greed, puts on his wife the burden of physical work outside the home jeopardizes his marriage and demonstrates his unfitness spiritually to rule his house well. A wife, as later lessons will show, is to be a worker at home (see 1 Tim. 5:14; Tit. 2:5). The exchanging of roles by husbands and wives in the home is a modern viewpoint, unknown to biblical teaching.

The physical needs of the wife also include sexual fulfillment. Sexual pleasure and satisfaction is one of the legitimate reasons for marriage. *"But, because of fornication,"* Paul wrote, *"let each man have his own wife, and let each woman have her own husband"* (1 Cor. 7:2). When God said at the beginning, *"they shall be one flesh,"* he spoke of the sexual union of the bodies of a man and a woman (Gen. 2:24). Although this oneness is immoral outside marriage (1 Cor. 6:16), it is respectable and pure between a husband and a wife. *"Let marriage be had in honor among all, and the bed be undefiled: for fornicators and adulterers God will judge"* (Heb. 13:4).

The apostle Paul portrays sexual relationship in marriage as a debt the husband owes his wife. *"Let the husband render unto the wife her due"* (1 Cor. 7:3). The word "render" means "to pay" and the term "due" means "a debt." A husband's sexual obligation to his wife is as definite as his house payment.

Paul takes this responsibility a step farther. *"The husband,"* he says, *"hath not power over his own body, but the wife"* (1 Cor. 7:4). The word "power" is the term that is often used to describe the "authority" of Christ. Matthew includes it in his account of the commission Jesus gave to the apostles. *"All power"* (KJV) or *"all authority"* (ASV), Jesus said, hath been given to me in heaven and on earth. The word means "rule" or "dominion" or "right to command." A wife, the term says, has dominion over her husband's body for her sexual needs.

Finally, the apostle says, *"Defraud ye not one the other, except it be by consent for a season"* (1 Cor. 7:5). "Defraud" means to "rob" and instructs a husband not to cheat his wife out of the debt he owes and the authority she has over his body. His body belongs to her and must not be withheld by him when she has need.

God unquestionably designed man and woman to be attractive and pleasurable to one another sexually. This is obvious from the fleshly lusts they feel for each other and from the problem of immorality that plagues every generation. Solomon, as the writer of Hebrews (Heb. 13:4), extols this pleasure in marriage and warns against its abuse with strangers (Prov. 5:10-16; see also Song of Solomon 5:10-16). A loving husband, however, is careful in seeking sexual pleasure not to damage the emotional stability of his wife.

3. Emotional Needs. A caring husband understands his wife's emotional needs. The body of woman, a husband must remember, is attached to her head. When seeking sexual pleasure for themselves, men frequently forget that physical and emotional satisfaction are inseparable. The two are intwined. A loving husband will avoid treating his wife as a "toy" to be used and then coldly set aside until he is ready to play again. The emotional needs of a woman cannot be met unless in the arms of her husband she feels like a person who is valued and respected.

This need is met by a husband who appreciates his wife beyond his lust for sexual pleasure. He treats her kindly during her monthly cycle or at times of low esteem before or after her cycle. When sex is not the object and he gives her attention, she knows she is more than a body to him. A husband gives meaning to the person of his wife and promotes her emotional health when he shows his love at all times.

Emotional Support

For the man who appreciates the willingness of his wife to stand against the tide of public opinion — staying at home in her empty neighborhood in the exclusive company of jelly-faced toddlers and strong willed adolescents — it is about time you gave her some help. I'm not merely suggesting that you wash the dishes or sweep the floor. I'm referring to the provision of emotional support . . . of conversation . . . of making her feel like a lady . . . of building her ego . . . of giving her one day of recreation each week . . . of taking her out to dinner . . . of telling her that you love her. Without these armaments, she is left defenseless against the foes of the family — the foes of *your* family! (pp. 102,103)

— **James C. Dobson,** *Straight Talk to Men and Their Wives*

When considering the emotional needs of woman, a husband must learn the value of words. Words like: "You are important to me"; "You are number one in my life"; "You are doing a good job"; "I appreciate you"; "May I help you with that?"; "I love you"; etc. Other important phrases are: "I am sorry"; "I was wrong"; "I will try"; "Please, forgive me." Meaningful expressions must not be limited to times of lovemaking when sexual pleasure is the object. Verbal love is an important ingredient in the daily social fare loving husbands supply their wives and does not stick in the crawl as utterances that reflect unfavorably on manliness.

4. Social Needs. Yes, caring husbands, wives have social needs. When a wife has spent eight to ten hours a day changing diapers, wiping snotty noses, settling arguments between children, bumping heads with a strong-willed child, cleaning up mess after mess, washing dishes, scrubbing floors, running kids to one event after another — she needs some relaxation, adult companionship, and some reassurances. And what she needs cannot come from her mother or father, a thoughtful neighbor, or an understanding sister in the Lord. It must come from the one man she chose over all other men to be her friend for life. A loving husband knows this and makes time for her: time to visit with her, take her out for dinner, get away with her for a weekend, or anything else that will bring the two together alone. What she does't need day after day is a muley, silent, indifferent couch potato who utters an occasional spaced-out groan or grunt.

Conclusion

The rule of a husband over his wife is a solemn and exacting role assigned by God. It calls for men — real men who seek to measure up to the love and compassion that Christ had for the church. What is not needed are totalitarian dictators who revel in their authority, who boast of manliness that tramples mercilessly upon weaker vessels, who rule with iron fists to the emotional destruction of loving companions, and who lay down heavy burdens to the hurt of fragile and delicate helpmates. A wife and family need a man who rules out of love, who rejoices in the wife of his youth, who honors her as a worthy mate, who understands her as a person with needs, and who sets her happiness above his desires.

The wife of a husband who, after the likeness of Christ, rules benevolently will have no difficulty accepting him as "head," "lord," or "ruler" of the home. She will gladly crown him "king" of her heart and life.

An Outline Study Guide

Introduction:

A. Discuss animosity toward men by feminists and list factors that may have contributed to this. _____

_____

B. How are husbands like corporate presidents?_____

_____

How prominent is the "slavery view" of wives as seen in the Silverstein song?

_____

I. Head of Wife:

A. To whom is a husband's rule compared (Eph. 5:23)?_____

What is another term to describe Christ's rule (2 Tim. 2:21; 2 Pet. 2:1)?

_____

Define it. _____

B. What did Sarah call Abraham (1 Pet. 3:6)?_____

What kind of lord is a husband?_____

_____

C. As ruler with all authority what is the goal of Jesus' rule of the church (Matt. 11:28-30; 5:1-12)? _____

_____

D. As head and ruler of the household how are men to approach their rule (Eph. 5:23)?_____

_____

Cite examples of how husbands put themselves ahead of their wives:

_____ , _____ , _____

II. Honor The Wife:

A. What does "honor" the wife mean (1 Pet. 3:7)?_____

_____

What do the Proverbs say about the value of the wife (Prov. 31:10; 18:22)?

_____

B. What did the husband of the worthy woman do (Prov. 31:28)?_____

_____

III. Hear The Wife:

A. What is the first goal of a husband's rule?_____

_____

What does Peter say about it (1 Pet. 3:7)?_____

B. What did Joshua decide for his family (Josh. 24:15)?_____

_____

What is said about the house of Stephanas (1 Cor. 16:15)?_____

_____

C. What is the first physical need of a wife (Gen. 3:19)?_____

_____

What is the chief role of the wife (1 Tim. 5:14; Tit. 2:5)?_____

_____

D. What physical and emotional needs do wives have (1 Cor. 7:2)?_____

_____

Should there be guilt feelings about his relationship (Heb. 13:4)?_____

_____

E. What do the words "due," "authority," and "defraud" say about sexual relations (1 Cor. 7:1-6)?_____

_____

F. Should men seek the pleasure of their wives (Prov. 5:10-16; Song of Solomon 5:10-16)? _____

_____

How might they damage their wives emotionally through sex?_____

_____

G. List and discuss ways husband's can meet their wives' social needs.____

_____

Specify one reason she has this need from him._____

_____

Conclusion:
A. Summarize ways husbands can practice the rule of love._____

_____

B. Summarize ways he can violate it._____

_____

Be in Subjection

Introduction

The word "subjection," when denoting the wife's relationship to her husband, conjures up images of slavery in the minds of today's feminists. A woman's submission to her husband is, women "libbers" believe, a token of inferiority and inequality. The role of subjection, they assert, relegates the wife to sub-human and second-class status in the family. Such charges arise from ignorance, misunderstanding, and distortion of God's design for women in marriage.

That the word "subjection" or the role of subjection makes no statement regarding inferiority or superiority is evident in the business world. Employees, for example, are subject to their employers, but are often more intelligent and more talented than their bosses. And surely they are not sub-human or second-class citizens because someone rules them. Roles, whether of submission or dominion, say nothing of themselves about ability or value. They speak only of functions and responsibilities.

The wife's role of subjection in marriage is assigned by God and must not be mistaken as a comment on her value or significance in God's plan for the family or society. When her place in the family is understood, her role in society will be magnified as basic and worthy. Her importance far transcends all the "free," career-chasing, egocentric women who accomplish little more than making money and satisfying their inflated egos.

The Most Important Job

What is easily the most important job in the world? The most important job of all is not doctor, lawyer, banker, or any of the other 25,000 occupations listed by the Census Bureau. The most important of all endeavors is the one that masquerades under the title of "housewife." Not only important, essential. From the Stone Age to the Space Age the wife and mother — the homemaker, the housewife — has kept the fires of civilization burning brightly and made this a better world for all of us (p. 16).

— **Dr. David Reubin** *via The Challenge of Being a Wife*

Basis of Subjection

The wife's role of subjection originates with the divine order of relationships as God assigned them. Society could not exist without order and the order God arranged is unmistakeable. With no particular reference to marriage God says: *"But I would have you know, that the head of every man is Christ; and the head of the woman is the man; and the head of Christ is God"* (1 Cor. 11:3). The apostle Paul further explains the divine order.

> For the man is not of the woman; but the woman of the man: for neither was the man created for the woman; but the woman for the man: for this cause ought the woman to have a sign of authority on her head, because of the angels (1 Cor. 11:8-10).

Noting the same reason for woman's subjection in another passage, Paul then adds: *"And Adam was not beguiled, but the woman being beguiled hath fallen into transgression"* (1 Tim. 2:12-14). Because the woman was deceived when the two sinned in the beginning God said to Eve: *"And thy desire shall be to thy husband, and he shall rule over thee"* (Gen. 3:16).

What must be especially emphasized about teaching concerning the wife's submission is that nothing is said or implied about inferiority or inequality. Such thoughts miss the point. Many wives are clearly superior to their husbands — intellectually, educationally, emotionally, spiritually, and socially. Subjection is simply the role God assigned her in the home. All relationships need leaders and followers and in the family the husband is the "head" and the wife is to be in "subjection."

Wives Be in Subjection

What exactly do the Scriptures say about the subjection of wives to their husbands? Remember, first of all, the marriage law itself speaks of leaving father and mother and cleaving to one another (Gen. 2:24). The wife, therefore, must leave the rule of her parents. Father and mother no longer have priority over her life. She must as a wife accept with a willing mind the new relationship God assigns her.

The wife's relationship in marriage is stated in almost identical language in three places. *"Wives, be in subjection to your own husbands"* (1 Pet. 3:1; Col. 3:18; Eph. 5:22). In Ephesians and Colossians the phrases *"as unto the Lord"* and *"as is fitting unto the Lord"* are added.

1. The Word Subjection. Observe that subjection is taught. The word "subjection" is a military term that means "to rank under" and denotes an order of roles. The role of the husband is to rule and the role of the wife is to submit. The wife's submission is compared to the church's relationship to Christ. *"But as the church is subject to Christ, so let the wives also be to their husbands in everything"* (Eph. 5:24).

Did not God know that at times a wife would see matters differently from her husband? Surely! But this is true of any relationship of rule or subjection. Yet, God chose to instruct wives to be in subjection to their husbands in *"everything."* A wife must, therefore, humble herself before God, respect his authority, and yield to the rule of her husband — even when her mind wants to say no. This does not forbid her to contribute ideas, nor does it tell her husband to dismiss her views; it only says that, as Sarah *"obeyed"* Abraham, she must obey her husband (1 Pet. 3:6).

2. The Word Obey. The word *"obeyed"* is translated from a Greek word that combines the prefix "under" with a verb "to hear." Thus obey means to bring oneself under what is heard. When the husband voices decisions for the family, the wife, according to Peter, is to listen and submit. Subjection, of course, is more difficult when a husband is unloving and uncaring, but is no less binding. A husband as a selfish leader is no reason for the wife to be a rebellious follower. A God-fearing wife vows to obey her husband and will keep that vow, as her foremother Sarah did. Sarah understood both Abraham's and her God-assigned roles and consented to them. She initiated no campaign for "rights," but accepted "responsibilities."

Do It Yourself (?)
In the 1980's we are sometimes seeing an up-date on the "Do-it-yourself craze" of earlier years. If a husband asks his wife to do something she says, "Do it yourself." In Genesis 18:6 Abraham said to Sarah, *"Make ready quickly three measures of fine meal, knead it, and make cakes."* Can you imagine Sarah answering, "Do it yourself"? This attitude would have been out of character for her for *"Sarah obeyed Abraham, calling him Lord"* (1 Pet. 3:6) (p. 51).

— **Darlene Craig,** *A Worthy Woman*

One exception clause, however, is attached to the wife's role of subjection. *"As unto the Lord"* and *"as is fitting in the Lord"* are expressions that set limits on the wife's subjection. The head of the man is Christ, as previously noted, and no husband has the authority to rule his wife in conflict with the teaching of *his* head. Christ has *"all authority"* (Matt. 28:18) and no wife is required to submit to dictates that violate her obedience to Christ. Christ is always number one in her heart.

This presents problems for a wife who is married to a non-Christian or an unfaithful Christian. That wives must submit to unbelieving husbands is not questioned. Peter settled that. *"In like manner, ye wives, be in subjection to your own husbands; that, even if any obey not the word, they may without the word be gained by the behavior of their wives; beholding your chaste behavior coupled with fear"* (1 Pet. 3:1,2). But what is she to do if he insists that she drink and dance, miss worship, deceive, dress immodestly, etc.? She must refuse. She is to be chaste. She must always behave herself *"as is fitting in the Lord."*

A faithful wife is always subject to the Lord first and her husband second. She, both in relation to Christ and her husband, submits to principle, not her own wisdom. She may not inject her views to violate the law of Christ or to rebel against the rule of her husband. In all things she must submit to her husband as unto the Lord. Acknowledging the authority of both Christ and her husband, she will serve reverently and humbly.

Qualities that Produce Subjection
When an ideal husband loves his wife as Christ loved the church, his wife has little difficulty submitting to him. In the words of one wife, "I wouldn't mind submitting to you if you were like Christ" *(Marriage: Agony and Ecstasy,* Helen Good Brenneman, p. 70). But how can she submit to a selfish, immature, unappreciative, unattentive, uncaring, demeaning husband? She, to begin with, submits in hopes that by prayer and service the beauty of her character will influence him to honor and love her.

1. Fear of God. The real power, however, that enables a wife to honor her husband's rule comes from the Lord. Subjection to an unfit husband grows out of a wife's "fear" or "reverence" for God. *"Grace is deceitful, and beauty is vain; but a woman that feareth Jehovah, she shall be praised"* (Prov. 31:30). A wife's subjection is founded not simply on her belief that God is, but on reverent commitment to him and his word. She worships his very Being and her subjection reflects devotion to his way. She believes he is infinitely wise and, thus, feels no reluctance toward managing the house and working at home in subjection to her husband, as God has authorized (1 Tim. 5:14; Tit. 2:5).

The reverence of a wife for God translates into "fear" of her husband. Again, because God commands it. *"And let the wife see that she fear her husband"* (Eph. 5:33). The word "fear" means to "revere" or "respect," as some versions translate it. It is the term used to describe man's attitude toward God (Acts 10:2) and denotes the esteem or high estimate a wife is to have for her husband's role. Respect for her husband, as reverence for God, produces subjection.

2. Meek and Quiet Spirit. Another quality that yields the subjection God commands is a *"meek and quiet spirit"* (1 Pet. 3:4). The word "meek" denotes a submissive spirit that surrenders itself to the control of a leader. Aristotle used the term of a horse whose will is broken and, as a result, submits to the reins of his master. So Peter describes devoted wives toward God and their husbands. He says her meekness *"is in the sight of God of great price"* (1 Pet. 3:4). It is part of the *"incorruptible apparel"* that adorns the heart of an obedient wife. The apostles relate this spirit to subjection:

> For after this manner aforetime the holy women also, who hoped in God, adorned themselves, being in subjection to their own husbands: as Sarah obeyed Abraham, calling him lord: whose children ye now are, if ye do well and are not put in fear by any terror (1 Pet. 3:5,6).

3. Holiness. Peter's words likewise show that holy women who hope in God are women who live in subjection to their husbands. The word *"holy"* means not only "set apart" from sin, but "consecrated" to righteousness. The heart of a woman trained by God's teaching, empowered by faith in his authority, and moved by consecration to his will takes seriously the role of subjection he assigned her in marriage. Subjection to her husband reflects holiness toward God.

4. Love. Finally, godly women submit to their husbands because they are taught in God's word to love their husbands and their children. *"Aged women,"* Paul wrote, are to *"train the young women to love their husbands, to love their children, to be . . . kind"* (Tit. 2:3-5). Loving women have learned to care for others and to give themselves for the good of their households. They view themselves as helpers suitably designed by God (see Gen. 2:18) to assist their husbands in reaching God's goals for the family. They, as a result, feel no competitive spirit to challenge their husbands for control of the home.

The worthy woman portrayed by Lemuel in Proverbs 31 is the ideal example for women of all times. She is described, first of all, as a woman who doeth her husband *"good and not evil all the days of her life"* (v. 12). He then details her industrious ways on behalf of the family: she *"worketh willingly with her hands"; "riseth also while it is yet night, and giveth food to her household"; "layeth her hands to the distaff, and her hands hold the spindle"; "looketh well to the ways of her household"* (vv. 13,15,19,27). Worthy women care about their husbands and families and see themselves as valuable workers in the home.

Conclusion

Subjection is understood and appreciated by folks who know the joy of serving. Christianity itself is based on self-denial and service (see Lk. 9:23; Matt. 20:20-28). Jesus awards greatness for service in his kingdom and promises — *"peace of God, which passeth all understanding"* and *"joy unspeakable"* (Phil. 4:6; 1 Pet. 1:8). Spirit-filled Christians empowered by the gospel know this joy and have no quarrel with subjection or service (see Rom. 1:16; Eph. 3:14-20; Gal. 5:22,23). Wives, therefore, who know the Lord assent to the role of subjection and joyfully serve their families.

Wives who willingly accept this role should not be viewed as brainless fools — incapable of decision-making and in need of someone to oversee them for their own safety. Managing the household, as the next lesson will discuss, is an important and challenging role. To do this job well — economically, orderly, smoothly — requires the genius of the most capable executive. A housewife need not blush or shrink back from admitting the career she has chosen and the subjection to which she is committed.

A submissive wife is a worthy woman, has accepted a worthy role, is committed to a worthy objective, and is performing a worthy work. She deserves the praise of her family, the gratitude of her nation, and the honor of any civilized society. May her husband treat her kindly and may God bless her richly.

An Outline Study Guide

Introduction:

A. What images does the word "subjection" conjure up?_____

_____

   Why does subjection say nothing about ability per se?_____

_____

   Illustrate your answer in the business world._____

_____

B. Who assigned woman this role and how does its value compare to a career?

_____

I. Basis of Subjection:

A. Outline the divine order of authority (1 Cor. 11:3)!_____,

   _____ , _____ , _____

B. State two reasons for this subjection (1 Cor. 11:8-10; 1 Tim. 2:12-14; Gen. 3:16):_____

_____

_____

II. Wives Be In Subjection:

A. What is the place of "in-laws" after marriage (Gen. 2:24)?_____

_____

   Unto whom is the wife to be in subjection (1 Pet. 3:1)?_____

_____

B. What qualifying phrases does Paul use about subjection (Eph. 5:22; Col. 3:18)?_____

C. Define the word "subjection."_____
   To what is subjection compared (Eph. 5:24)? _____

D. Define "obey" and note who it described (1 Pet. 3:6)._____

E. To whom is the wife ultimately subject (Matt. 28:18)?_____

   Note problems this may present with ungodly husbands._____

III. Qualities That Produce Subjection:
A. State a practical reason for submitting to unloving husbands._____

B. What is the real reason wives submit (Prov. 31:30)?_____

   Does this mean they will be homemakers (1 Tim. 5:14; Tit. 2:5)?_____
   Why?_____

C. What is a godly woman's attitude about her husband (Eph. 5:33)?_____
   Define "fear":_____

D. What spirit must a wife possess (1 Pet. 3:4)?_____
   Name two attributes of her spirit:_____
   What is meant by "meek" and how does it relate to subjection?_____

E. How do "holiness" and "love" bring about subjection (1 Pet. 3:5; Tit. 2:4)?_____

F. How was the "worthy" woman's attitude manifested toward her family (Prov. 31:12,14,15,19,17)? _____

Conclusion:
A. How does subjection relate to the basics of the gospel (Lk. 9:23; Matt. 20:20-28)?_____

B. What reward comes from subjection that serves in the kingdom (Phil. 4:6; 1 Pet. 1:8)? _____

C. Review: State ways husbands are subject to wives — to meet their needs and serve them out of love (Gen. 3:19; 1 Cor. 7:1-6; Eph. 5:25-29)?_____

_____

D. Why would you say housewifing is not a brainless job?_____

_____

E. Why is being a housewife an important role in the home and society?_____

_____

A Help Meet

Introduction

And Jehovah God said, It is not good that the man should be alone; I will make him a *help meet* for him. . . And Jehovah God caused a deep sleep to fall upon the man, and he slept; and he took one of his ribs, and he closed up the flesh instead thereof: and the rib, which Jehovah God had taken from the man, made he a woman, and brought her unto the man. And the man said, This is now bone of my bones, and flesh of my flesh: she shall be called Woman, because she was taken out of the man (Gen. 2:18,21-23).

When man stood alone before Jehovah at the time of creation, he lacked something vital to his being, to the ongoing of the human race, and to the needs of an upcoming society. God had formed every beast of the field and every bird of the heavens, but in none of them was help suitable for the ultimate purpose of creation (see Gen. 2:19,20). Out of man's flesh and bones God designed a special creature whom the man himself called — "woman." She was prepared uniquely to complete what was lacking in the man and to make him a total being. Her duties consist primarily of fulfilling the role of helper to man.

The place of helper to man is not one to be taken lightly. It must not be viewed by the husband or the wife as the role of a lackey. Wives, as previously noted, are to be in subjection to their husbands but that does not suggest inferiority, inequality, or second-class status in the family or society. As helper to her husband the woman's responsibilities as a wife are specifically spelled out. That must now be examined.

A Help Meet

God, according to the opening text, created woman when there was not found in all creation *"a help meet"* for man. The two terms *"help"* and *"meet"* are vital to understanding the relationship of a wife to her husband. The word *"help"* means to aid or assist, denoting God's design for the woman to support the man. Whatever the husband's role is and whatever the family goals are, the woman is to help bring those to fulfillment. That man needs help testifies to his insufficiency without woman. God, in other words, demands responsibilities of man that he alone cannot perform. A wife, in this respect, must see herself in some roles as superior to her husband — created special to function in ways he cannot. A godly woman views these roles as monuments to her unique qualities.

The definition of *"meet"* is literally "over against" and means to answer to, to correspond to, or to be suitable for. Woman, the thought is, was produced from the same kind of mold as man, but was made opposite to him to fit together with his being much like two pieces of a jigsaw puzzle. She was bone of his bones and flesh of his flesh and was made *from* the man *for* the man (Gen. 2:23; 1 Cor. 11:8,9). What the animal kingdom was unable to do for man, God designed woman to accomplish. The goal of this lesson is to observe the suitability of woman as a wife to meet the personal and family needs of the man as a husband. Her role as mother must be studied in a later lesson.

Be Fruitful

The most basic example of the suitability of woman as a helper to man is the responsibility assigned the two to *"be fruitful, and multiply, and replenish the earth"* (Gen. 1:28). Animals, it is clear, are not capable of helping man produce offspring. Woman, it is just as obvious, is fashioned perfectly for this purpose. As a wife she can join herself to her husband as one flesh and fulfill the function of *"child-bearing"* (1 Tim. 2:15). This unique ability is distasteful and demeaning to some modern feminists, but it is a role assigned by God that only woman can fulfill. Holy women accept this duty and see it as a rewarding, satisfying, integral part of their God-ordained mission in life. It completes what man cannot do alone, and women of faith accept this honorable role with joy and gratification. Nothing expresses so vividly the opposite yet complementary natures of man and woman — as does the union of their two bodies to produce the offspring of a new generation.

Companionship

Previous lessons have noted and it must be repeated here that *"it is not good that the man should be alone"* (Gen. 2:18). Again, the animal world offered nothing suitable to fulfill man's need for a friend. Dog is not man's best friend. Despite the presence of hundreds of animals — domestic and wild — man was alone without a corresponding creature of his own likeness. Animals could not communicate with man intellectually to help him solve problems. Beasts could not rejoice with him and share as partners in the good fortunes of life. And neither birds nor snakes could weep and commiserate with man in the heartaches that come from his losses.

Man needed someone like himself. *"And God created man in his own image, in the image of God created he him; male and female created he them"* (Gen. 1:27). Man and woman are of like image and are, as a result, compatible to be friends, to be companions, to share life together. When companionship fails and walls of silence go up, friendship and communication break down and a vital need of man is not met. Tragedy cannot be far behind when the loneliness of man is not dispelled by the unique ability God gave woman to fill that void.

Talk to widowers about the importance of companionship. It is not the absence of sexual satisfaction, not the need for a housekeeper, and not the lack of a cook that make the days long and the nights at times unbearable. His "aloneness" and his need for companionship dominate his thoughts and, in some cases, drive him up the wall. He can become so utterly empty and starved for the friendship he once knew that he explodes with tears and crying to his Lord. The emotional bond that blends two hearts and lives together as one is fundamental to the completeness of man and woman.

Wives who are too busy to be companions to their husbands have a scheduling or priority problem. The needs of children must be met, PTA meetings are important, shopping and following garage sales are fine, time at the health spa is relaxing and wholesome, coffee clutches can be enjoyable and stimulating, a job in some instances is necessary, keeping in contact with mama is all right, and Bible study, visiting the sick and personal work are absolutes. If, however, a wife is cumbered with these things to the neglect of her husband's need for emotional support through companionship, she has failed in a basic role assigned by God.

Wives must communicate with their husbands — talk to them about their day, listen to their problems, rejoice with them in their successes, support them when they have failed, express their opinions when asked, laugh at their jokes, touch or hold them when stress or contemplation has produced silence. Devoted wives seek to understand their husbands and their moods. They work in their unique way to satisfy the deep need of their spirits for a friend and a companion.

Advice From The Other Woman

Dear Woman: Your husband became greatly enamored of me because I paid attention to him, which obviously you haven't done in quite some time. I mean *real* attention, complete with stimulating conversation and verbal recognition of his extraordinary qualities. I made him feel alive and important. He believes you prefer the company of your sisters, your mothers and your women friends to him. When you need a man's viewpoint you ask your father.

I am not going to see your husband again, lady, because he likes me too much already, and I am no homewrecker. But I believe you should take a good, hard look at that wonderful man of yours and come up with some evidence of appreciation — before you lose him (pp. 68,69).

— **Letter to Ann Landers** *via The Challenge of Being a Wife*

Affection

Man's emotional needs reach beyond the bounds of friendship into the more intimate area of affection. Men often play the "macho" role and mask their need for expressions of tenderness. But they need affection and God knew it. The apostle Paul ordered evangelists to teach older women to *"train the young women to love their husbands, to love their children"* (Tit. 2:4). Yes, husbands need love just as surely as little children do.

Praise Versus Criticism

In order to understand this, it is important to know that the husband too needs the feeling of being sheltered. This feeling is conveyed to him if his wife makes an effort to understand him, to participant in the problems of his work, as if she were in his place. If she does this, she will always find something in his work which is worthy of praise which she can express to him. Few women realize how much a man is dependent upon the affirmation and acknowledgement of a woman. Nothing "conquers" him more than being praised by a woman. And if he receives more praise from another woman than from his wife, this may be the first step toward infidelity.

On the other hand, mockery and degrading criticism are poison for the male ego, which is often more vulnerable than the female ego. When criticism and failures have beaten him down all day, he comes home deflated, like a tire without air. Never does he long more for affirmation from his wife than in this moment. Through her praise she has to pump him into shape again (pp. 27,28).

— **Ingrid Trobisch,** *The Joy of Being a Woman*

The word for love in this verse is *phileo,* which is not so much "devoted care" as *agapao,* but affection or tender feeling. Husbands, as wives, need to hear: "I love you"; "You are important to me"; "I appreciate you"; "You are doing a good job"; "I need you." A man's self-esteem is important and needs to be bolstered by expressions of love. A husband wants to be admired, needs to know his worth, and yearns for esteem from his wife. Man longs for compliments from his boss and close friends, but craves most of all the emotional support of an affectionate wife. Charlie Shedd gave this advice to his daughter Karen regarding her husband: "You can keep him loving you for ever if you learn a thousand different ways to tell him he's wonderful" *(Letters to Karen,* p. 42). That affection will also be expressed with hugs and kisses and attention to his sexual needs.

Sexual Needs

Since, as noted in another lesson, the head is attached to the body, affection and emotional needs blend imperceptibly with physical or sexual urges. Affection of a wife for her husband reaches out for the *"one flesh"* relationship which is vital to the completion of man (see Gen. 2:24; Matt. 19:5; Heb. 13:4). The union of their bodies as one is the most intimate and most obvious way a wife corresponds to her husband's needs. She is perfectly designed for this role.

Although a husband and his wife join their bodies to *"multiply, and replenish the earth"* (Gen. 1:28), it is false to conclude, as some have, that this oneness is never intended strictly for the pleasure of the husband and the wife. Solomon clearly highlights sexual satisfaction as a goal of the *"one flesh"* relationship (see Prov. 5:15-20; Song of Solomon 5:10-16). The women's liberation movement, if it has accomplished nothing else, has corrected the false notion that sexual union is only for the pleasure of men. The joy of sex is for both man and woman. The wife who understands this will relax and seek with pleasure to satisfy the needs of her husband.

It is necessary to repeat for the wives what has already been said to husbands. *"But, because of fornication, let each man have his own wife, and let each woman have her own husband"* (1 Cor. 7:2). Women and men both have sexual desires and, to avoid immorality, are to meet one another's needs. Each is to enjoy the pleasure of the other's body within marriage (see Heb. 13:4).

Paul, then, says to wives what he says to husbands. The wife is to *"render"* unto the husband his *"dues"* (1 Cor. 7:3). These two words obligate the wife to meet her husband's sexual needs as a debt to be paid. The apostle, next, says: *"The wife hath not power over her body, but the husband"* (1 Cor. 7:4). The word "power" is the word for "authority" (Matt. 28:18) that depicts the right of Christ to rule the lives of all men. The husband, thus, has dominion or rule of the wife's body for the fulfillment of his desire for sex. Finally, Paul says: *"Defraud ye not one the other, except it be by consent for a season"* (1 Cor. 7:5). The wife must not, as the word "defraud" means, cheat or rob her husband of sexual pleasure.

As *"one flesh"* with her husband, a dedicated wife finds pleasure for herself, seeks to provide pleasure for her husband, and zealously gives herself to this duty. She is suitably designed physically and emotionally for this task and must not let any distortion of this role hinder the completion that she alone can lawfully supply her husband.

Keepers At Home

Two words are used in Scripture to underscore one other way woman was suitably created to help man. The first one, *oikodespotes,* means literally "house-ruler." It combines the Greek word for "house" with the Greek word for "despot" or "ruler." Speaking of young widows, Paul wrote to Timothy:

> And withal they learn also to be idle, going about from house to house; and not only idle, but tattlers also and busybodies, speaking things which they ought not. I desire therefore that the younger widows marry, bear children, *rule the household,* give no occasion to the adversary for reviling (1 Tim. 5:13,14).

"Keeping house" (NASB) and "manage their homes" (NIV) are two other translations given to the phrase "rule the household." God, unquestionably, planned for woman to take charge of the house, a reference, as is evident in the example of the worthy woman, to the domestic responsibilities of cooking, sewing, cleaning, etc. (see Prov. 31:10-31). This is also clear in the word *oikourgos,* a second word used by Paul. It combines the words "work" and "house." When writing to Titus Paul told older women to train young woman to be *"workers at home"* (Tit. 2:5, "keepers at home," KJV). While man is to work by the sweat of his face to provide for the family (see Gen. 3:19), his wife is to be his helper by working in the home.

Lemuel depicts the worthy woman as a dedicated domestic. She arises early to prepare meals for the family (v. 15), she spins yarn that is woven into carpets and cloth for garments (vv. 19,22,14), and she looketh well to the ways of her household (v. 27). No work is any more important or central to the health of family relations than the work God assigned woman in the home. Love is imparted in the direct and personal giving of woman in the midst of the household, security is derived from the stability of her daily presence there, and training is permitted by the quantity of time she can offer. Ask any child who is greeted with a kiss from mama and a jar of fresh baked cookies when he arrives home from school. Ask any husband who greets his wife with a peck on the lips amidst the aroma of tasty home cooking. Ask either of them about love, security, warmth — about what really matters and has real worth to a family.

Why would anyone label this work "menial" or "demeaning"? A wife in the home is a co-partner with her husband in family life. What she provides in the home is as significant as what he provides from outside the home. Both are giving themselves to God-ordained roles and neither should be ashamed. No woman need feel ashamed, inferior, subhuman, or second-class for taking seriously the wholesome tasks in the home — labors of love around which the family is unified and bonded to together.

Conclusion

What wives must remember is that man stood at the beginning — alone, insufficient, incomplete. He needed a helper in his own image who was competent to supply what was lacking. God made a special, unique creature to fill this need, brought her to man, and man called her "woman." She can be either good or bad for man — depending on how well she fulfills the role God assigned her. Many have, as Sarah, the Worthy Woman, or Priscilla, obeyed their husbands, shared life with them, and complemented their work (Gen. 18:1-8; Prov. 31:10-31; Acts 18:1-4, 24-28). Others have, as Eve, Jezebel, or Sapphira, dominated their husband for evil, condoned their evil devices, and frustrated the goals of family life (Gen. 3:1-8; 1 Kgs. 19:1,2; 21:1-16;

Acts 5:1-5). It is all a matter of her dedication to God and how seriously she takes the role God assigned her as a *"help meet"* for her husband.

An Outline Study Guide

Introduction:

A. Why did God make a help meet for man (Gen. 2:18)?_____

_____

B. What are some functions animals were not suitable to supply?_____

_____

I. Help Meet:

A. State the two key words in Genesis 2:18._____

What does "help" denote? _____

_____

B. Define "meet": _____

What does "from" man and "for" man say about woman's role (Gen. 2:23; 1 Cor. 11:8,9)?_____

_____

II. Be Fruitful:

A. What is the most basic example of woman's suitability (Gen. 1:28)?____

_____

What word does Paul use to describe this function (1 Tim. 2:15)?_____

_____

B. Why was pain added to this duty (Gen. 3:16)?_____

_____

III. Companionship:

A. What indicated man's need for companionship (Gen. 2:18)?_____

_____

B. Cite things that interfere with a wife's role of companion to her husband

_____

State also ways she can fulfill this role_____

_____

IV. Affection:

A. What did Paul say about wives' affection for their husbands (Tit. 2:4)?

_____

What word does Paul use here for love and what does it mean?_____

_____

B. Why do you agree with Charlie Shedd's advice that a wife should tell her husband she loves him in a thousand different ways?_____

Why do men need this kind of emotional support?_____

_____

Give reasons or examples for your answer._____

_____

V. Sexual Needs:
A. Who may legitimately enjoy the pleasures of sex (Gen. 2:24; Heb. 13:4)?

_____

Can sex be strictly for physical pleasure (1 Cor. 7:1,2)?_____

_____

B. Review: What do the words "due," "power," and "defraud" say about the wife's duty to her husband sexually (1 Cor. 7:3-5)?_____

_____

VI. Keepers At Home:
A. What does *oikodespotes* mean? _____

Where is it used?_____

What responsibilities would this include?_____

B. Define *oikourgos*. _____

Where is it found? _____

C. Detail some tasks the "worthy" woman accepted (Prov. 31:15,19,22,21,27).

_____

D. What merits are there for being a housewife? _____

_____

Conclusion:
A. Cite and discuss examples of women who were valuable helpers to their husbands (Gen. 18:1-8; Prov. 31:10-31; Acts 18:1-4,24-28)._____

_____

B. Cite and discuss examples of women who were hindrances to their husbands (Gen. 3:1-8; 1 Kgs. 19:1,2; 21:1-16; Acts 5:1-5)._____

_____

_____

Train Up a Child

Introduction

The word "parent" is derived from a Latin root that means "bring forth" or "beget." It described originally the biological and physical process by which husbands and wives gave birth to children. Every parent knows, however, that there is much more to "parenting" than the ability to bear an offspring. Nothing, in fact, is quite as awesome as knowing that the destiny of a precious life, the life of a child, almost entirely depends on whether one as a father or mother fulfills the role that God has given parents.

This responsibility is stated so simply, and yet so poignantly, in the familiar proverb: *Train up a child in the way he should go, And even when he is old he will not depart from it* (Prov. 22:6).

Three thoughts are taught in this verse about children. First, there is a way children should or ought to go. The number one issue that must be settled for children is the question of right and wrong. The call of the world is strong and a diabolical worldview tugs at the heart strings of today's youth. The appeal is sounded forth in school textbooks, TV and movies, and much of the popular print media. Spurred by the evolutionary hypothesis that man is merely a higher form of animal, humanism seeks with evangelistic zeal to capture the minds of young people. The philosophy puts man at the center of the universe and urges him to trust his own heart in search of truth. Parents, the ones responsibile for this training, must resolve that God's teaching maps out *"the way"* their children *"should go."*

Second, training is essential if children are to go the way they should. Training involves both instruction and discipline. Youngsters must, therefore, receive the right information. They must be enlightened by God's teaching. Wisdom from above must be thoroughly and forcibly implanted into their thinking. They must likewise be corrected at wrong turns in the way. Restrictions of conduct must be lovingly, yet firmly, enforced. This, again, is the principal role of parents, not the church, the schools, or the media.

Finally, the proverb teaches that the most lasting impressions upon man are the trainings he received from his youth. Many studies today show that the love, holding, cuddling of a child in the very first hours and days are important to his emotional stability. Not only are early manifestations of love significant, but immediate expressions of control have a bearing on who rules the household. Some have boldly affirmed, and evidence backs them, that they can form a child's permanent principles and conduct in the first seven years of life. Solomon is not arguing the impossibility of change, but he is counseling those responsible for a child's training to make the early years count.

The proverb says nothing specifically about parents, but biblical teaching invariably points to fathers and mothers as the principal agents of this training. That parents in large measure have relinguished the control of children's minds to schools, churches, mass media, and fellow classmates or friends is indisputable. That this is a mistake for which society is paying and parents are wringing their hands is also evident. The solution is no less obvious. Parents must examine carefully and fulfill diligently the role that God assigned them in the home. What, then, does the Creator expect of husbands and wives who become fathers and mothers? He expects exactly what he commended in his faithful servant Abraham: *"For I have known him to the end that he may command his children and his household after him, that they may keep the way of Jehovah, to do righteousness and justice"* (Gen. 18:19).

Winning Early

When a parent loses the early confrontations with the child, the later conflicts become harder to win. The parent who never wins, who is too weak or too tired or too busy to win, is making a costly mistake that will come back to haunt him during the child's adolescence. If you can't make a five-year-old pick up his toys, it is unlikely that you will exercise any impressive degree of control during his adolescence, the most defiant time of life. It is important to understand that adolescence is a condensation or composite of all the training and behavior that has gone before. Any unsettled matter in the first twelve years is likely to fester and erupt during adolescence (p. 33).

— **James C. Dobson,** *Dare to Discipline*

Love Their Children

To follow Abraham parents must love their children. Even humanistic psychologists recognize that early on children need affection. In what is now called "bonding," experts note that handling, hugging, and kissing of infants by parents are vital to healthy emotional development of children. Titus, a preacher, was instructed to *"speak thou the things which befit the sound doctrine,"* which included teaching older women to *"train the young women . . . to love their children"* (Tit. 2:3,4). The word "love" here means "affection" and describes both the devotion and displays of feelings parents must give children.

That children need affection from their parents is as basic as the nature of man himself. God knew, for example, that man who was alone at the beginning needed love. He, thus, created woman, in part, to fill that need. The emotional health of any person cries out for attention from others. Children not only need it as infants but as adolescents and adults. Parents cannot expect to succeed in commanding children in the way of Jehovah when they neglect the child in his most basic need — the need for love.

Love in its purest form is attention: playing with the child, listening to him, answering his questions, taking him to the store, buying his favorite treat, helping him with homework, showing interest in his hobbies, expressing feelings for him, telling him he is important, commending his worthy deeds, rebuking him in tenderness and firmness for his mistakes. Love is saying to children by teaching and actions that they are no bother, that they are important and father and mother like having them around.

Good Examples

Equally fundamental to the role of parents is good example. Note that Abraham commanded *"his children and his household after him."* This is not true merely in family life, but in any leadership role. Jesus, for example, saw in his work the need to leave man *"an example that ye should follow his steps"* (1 Pet. 2:21). Paul urged other Christians to follow him as he imitated Christ (1 Cor. 11:1). He also taught elders and preachers to take heed first to themselves (Acts 20:28; 1 Pet. 5:1-3; 1 Tim. 4:11-13,16).

Parents as examples call to mind a number of key biblical illustrations. First, the mother and grandmother of Timothy. Timothy was, of all of Paul's helpers, the most dedicated. Paul tells the Philippians that none of his fellow workers was as unselfishly devoted to their needs as Timothy (Phil. 2:19-22). When writing to Timothy himself, Paul noted his sincere faith *"which dwelt first in thy grandmother Lois, and thy mother Eunice"* (2 Tim. 1:5). Timothy as an evangelist walked by faith and cared spiritually for others, in part, because of what he observed as a child in his mother and grandmother. Parents who take their role seriously will not ignore the power of example in the life of this devoted evangelist.

But neither must fathers and mothers fail to notice the force of bad examples. Consider, for instance, the partiality of Isaac and Rebekah toward their sons — the father toward Esau and the mother toward Jacob (Gen. 25:28). Is it any wonder, then, that Jacob showed respect to Joseph and Benjamin over his other sons? A proverb in Israel stated it succinctly, *"As is the mother, so is her daughter"* (Ezek. 16:44). A modern saying puts it, "Like father, like son." A poem by an unknown author captures the thought vividly.

The Bad Example

He whipped his boy for lying,
  And his cheeks were flaming red,
And of course there's no denying
  There was truth in what he said —
That a liar's always hated.
  But the little fellow knew
That his father often stated
  Many things that were untrue.

He caught the youngster cheating
  And he sent him up to bed,
And it's useless now repeating
  All the bitter things he said,
He talked of honor loudly,
  As a lesson to be learned,
And forgot he's boasted proudly
  Of the curring tricks he's turned.

He heard the youngster swearing
  And he punished him again —

He'd have no boy as daring
As to utter words profane.
Yet the youngster could have told him,
Poor misguided little elf,
That it seemed unfair to scold him
When he often curses, himself.

All in vain is splendid preaching,
And the noble things we say,
All our task is wasted teaching
If we do not lead the way.
We can never, by reviewing
All the sermons on the shelves,
Keep the younger hands from doing
What we often do ourselves.
— **Author Unknown**

Parents who refuse to deny ungodly lusts and live unholy lives should not be amazed that their children as adults devote themselves to carnal appetites (see Tit. 2:12). Fathers and mothers who use the Lord's name in vain, tell suggestive and filthy jokes, gossip, lie and deceive should not be surprised when their children mimic their speech. Parents who only sporadically assemble with the saints, seldom read the Bible, are never known to pray, have no time to visit the elderly or sick should not be astonished when their children show no interest in spiritual activities.

Unforgiving attitudes, refusal to acknowledge wrongs, unwillingness to apologize, dual standards (one for parents and one for children), physical abuse and constant nagging, watching movies or TV shows that display explicit sex and use crude language are just a few of the unhealthy examples parents often set before their children. Fathers and mothers undermine the job of commanding their households *"to do righteousness"* when they refuse to walk that way themselves. Godly examples are the foundation for instruction and discipline that are vital to child training.

Nurture Children

Training children demands that parents, in the words of Paul, *"nurture them in the chastening and admonition of the Lord"* (Eph. 6:4). Remember, parents, the Lord did not give this responsibility to the church. Yes, the church is to teach all nations and preach the gospel to every creature. But what the church does in these matters is not a fulfillment of the duty God gave parents.

Nurturing and chastening children is directed to *"fathers."* Although the teaching of children is required of both fathers and mothers (Prov. 1:8; 6:20), the role of fathers must be emphasized. The reason? Fathers today have all but dumped this duty in the lap of mothers, a sad commentary on their perception of the obligation to "rule" the household. It was *Abraham* who commanded his household in the *"way of Jehovah."*

The word *"nurture"* means principally *"to nourish, promote health and strength."* The context of the above passage points to spiritual soundness and nourishment of the inner person. The term *"chastening"* denotes literally *"child training"* and refers to the rearing of children. Teaching, correcting, disciplining, loving are all elements of this responsibility. *"Admonition"* means *"to put in mind"* and highlights the importance of knowledge and understanding. All of this — nurturing, chastening and admonition — must be *"of the Lord."* Truth, the word of the Lord (Jn. 17:17) or the *"way of Jehovah"* (Gen. 18:14), is the guide for training children in the way they should go.

Paul urges Timothy to continue in what he learned as a child, an indirect commendation of the nurturing practice of Jewish parents. *"From a babe,"* he wrote, *"thou hast known the sacred writings which are able to make thee wise unto salvation through faith which is in Christ Jesus"* (2 Tim. 3:15). These Scriptures, he further notes, are *"profitable for teaching, for reproof, for correction, for instruction which is in righteousness"* (v. 16). Jewish fathers and mothers taught the Scriptures in the following manner:

> And these words, which I command thee this day, shall be upon thy heart; and thou shalt teach them diligently unto thy children, and shalt talk of them when thou sittest in thy house, and when thou walkest by the way, and when thou liest down, and when thou risest up (Deut. 6:6,7).

This is what parenting is all about. Conscientious parents spend long hours studying the Scriptures to prepare themselves for the task of teaching their children. It is they who must combat the atheistic, humanistic value system that grows out of the evolutionary hypothesis and denies basic biblical morality and ethics. Over and over and over, as this text indicates, fathers and mothers must drill, instill and fill their offsprings with the scriptural message of righteousness.

A steady diet of daily Bible study and prayer must be an integral part of family life. At the supper table, around the coffee table, before the fireplace, in the automobile the Scriptures must be read, analyzed, and applied. If children are to remain free from the garbage of secular values, parents must shut off the TV, bow in prayer with them, open the Bible, and take a little time each evening to teach them some spiritual truth. Do it, daddy and mama, when the children are babes and as adolescents they won't be embarrassed by it and it won't seem like "church stuff" that is out of place in the home.

Discipline Children

Teaching children is not enough. What is taught must also be enforced by discipline. Parents until recent years have known the value of saying "no" and punishing disobedient children. Many modern psychologists now see the error of the permissive approach to child training that dominated the past generation of parents. Believers in God have always known: *"He that spareth the rod hateth his son; But he that loveth him chastenenth him betimes"* (Prov. 13:24).

The writer of Hebrews discusses discipline in describing God's relationship to Christians (Heb. 12:5-11). He parallels God's role to the duty of parents. He says, number one, that God's discipline of his children proceeds out of love, out of *agape* (v. 6). Parents, accordingly, must discipline their children because they care, because a lesson vital to their well being is needed. When discipline, number two, issues out of love it promotes *"reverence"* (v. 9). Respect and subjection by children are the fruit of loving parental discipline. Harsh, unfair, and abusive treatment are what provoke wrath and bitterness in children (see Eph. 6:4; Col. 3:21). The peaceable fruit of righteousness is the third result of chastisement (v. 11). Children learn what is right and wrong and how to behave when discipline is properly administered.

Say "No" And Mean It

The other day I was sitting in a muffler shop, waiting for a new muffler to be put on our car. A young Mommi came in with Mark, about five years old, and plopped down two seats away from mine. After three minutes, Mark began to demand "a dwink," pointing to the pop machine.

"No, Mark," the Mommi said. But Mark knew, and I knew, by the way she said "no" that she really meant "keep pushing me and I'll give in." So Mark began his campaign. He threatened to hit her. He got on the floor and screamed. He accused her of not loving him. And he said some things that little Maxis or Marks should not say. It was too much.

I turned to the Mommi and said, "Please, for Mark's sake, discipline him! He will thank you for it later. Buy a copy of Dr. James Dobson's book, *Dare to Discipline* for Mark's sake and yours" (pp. 57,58).
— **Letter to Moody Monthly** *via Straight Talk to Men and Their Wives*

Eli was a loyal priest in Israel, but he put no reins on his children. Because *"he restrained them not,"* his sons hearkened not to his voice, defied the law of Moses, and indulged in the basest of fleshly lusts (1 Sam. 3:12-14; 2:22-25). Eli's failure as a father to control his sons speaks volumes to parents about the need of restrictions and discipline.

Conclusion

More needs to be said about fathers and mothers, but it must be left to later lessons. The basics of training children, the purpose of this lesson, are capsulized in the parental role of love, righteous example, instruction, and discipline. The next lesson will key in on specific principles children need to learn from their parents.

An Outline Study Guide

Introduction:

A. What is the original meaning of "parent"?_____

_____

Why is parenting much more awesome than this meaning?_____

_____

B. How does Solomon sum up the role of parents (Prov. 22:6)?_____

_____

C. What three ideas are found in Prov. 22:6?_____

_____

D. Summarize Abraham's training of his family (Gen. 18:19)._____

_____

I. Love Children:

A. What is fundamental to all child training?_____

Who are to teach this to young women (Tit. 2:3,4)?_____

   B. What is the purest form of love?_____

       Cite examples from the text and your own experience._____

       _____

II. Good Examples:
   A. What is said about Abraham's example (Gen. 18:19)?_____

       _____

       What other roles illustrate the need for example (1 Pet. 2:21; 1 Cor. 11:1; Acts 20:28; 1 Tim. 4:11-13,16)?_____

       _____

   B. How did example affect Timothy (2 Tim. 1:5; Phil. 2:19-22)?_____

       _____

       What resulted from Isaac and Rebekah's partiality (Gen. 25:28)?_____

       _____

       How does a Jewish proverb state it (Ezek. 16:44)?_____

       _____

III. Nurture Children:
   A. What does Paul say to parents about training (Eph. 6:4)?_____

       _____

       What parent is specifically addressed? _____
       Why does this need to be underscored?_____

       _____

   B. Define "nurture": _____
       "Chastening":_____
       "Admonition": _____
       What does "of the Lord" say about training?_____

       _____

   C. When did Timothy receive his training (2 Tim. 3:15)? _____

       _____

       From what was he trained (2 Tim. 3:15)? _____

       _____

   D. How did Jewish parents train their children (Deut. 6:6,7)? _____

       _____

IV. Discipline Children:
   A. What does Solomon say about punishing children (Prov. 13:24)?_____

       _____

   B. Out of what must discipline be administered (Heb. 12:6)?_____

       _____

What attitude does it produce (Heb. 12:9)?_____

What fruit will it produce (Heb. 12:11)?_____

C. What will abusive treatment of children produce (Eph. 6:4; Col. 3:21)?_

_____

What are examples of child abuse in your opinion?_____

_____

D. What is the principal way Eli failed his children (1 Sam. 3:12-14)?_____

_____

How did his sons act (1 Sam. 2:22-25)?_____

Conclusion:*
Capsulize each major point in the study and summarize the role of training children.

Honor Thy Parents

Introduction

The disposition children manifest toward their fathers and mothers is often a measure of the training they have received. A portion, therefore, of any adult study guide on family life must be devoted to the attitude parents are to instill in their offspring. No scene, for example, is quite as disgusting as a child's display of disdain and disrespect for his parents. To see a child sass, hit, or tell his father or mother to shut up is utterly nauseating. No behavior demands to be treated with any more seriousness and firmness.

This is not to say a child's viewpoint should not be heard and understood. It does say, though, that there is a correct way to address and to treat one's father and mother. What children say to their parents and how they say it should reflect honor and love and respect. And whether they possess these qualities is largely up to the parents.

> ### Answering The Call To Battle
>
> In my opinion, spankings should be reserved for the moment a child (age ten or less) expresses a defiant "I will not " or "You shut up!" When a youngster tries this kind of stiff-necked rebellion, you had better take it out of him, and pain is a marvelous purifier. When nose-to-nose confrontation occurs between you and your child, it is not the time to have a discussion about the virtues of obedience. It is not the occasion to send him to his room to pout. It is not appropriate to wait until poor, tired old dad comes plodding in from work, just in time to handle the conflicts of the day. You have drawn a line in the dirt, and the child has deliberately flopped his big hairy toe across it. Who is going to win? Who has the most courage? Who is in charge here? If you do not answer these questions conclusively for the child, he will precipitate other battles designed to ask them again and again. It is the ultimate paradox of childhood that a youngster wants to be controlled, but he insists that his parents earn the right to control him (pp. 27,28).
>
> — **James C. Dobson,** *Dare to Discipline*

Children who learn to *honor* their parents will *listen* to them, *obey* them, *praise* them, and *value* parental control and discipline. That fathers and mothers are instrumental in developing these attitudes and feelings is granted and will be emphasized. But children need to understand that, even if their parents fail, they are still responsible for these things.

Honor Thy Parents

When God delivered what some call the "preamble" to the law of Moses, He carved Ten Commandments in stone with his finger. The fifth of those commandments said:

Honor thy father and thy mother, that thy days may be long in the land which Jehovah thy God giveth thee (Exod. 20:12).

The apostle Paul, with slight variation, repeats this commandment in the New Testament (Eph. 6:2). The term *"honor"* means "to treat as a thing of value" or "to count as precious." Children's relationship to their fathers and mothers, as God designed it, starts with the perception of parental worth — worth as progenitors, providers, protectors, and instructors. Parents, though, must develop, demand, and enforce this viewpoint. Fathers and mothers who care about their children are adamantly intolerant of all signs of disrespect, dishonor, and rebellion.

Parents will take this stance if they respect the wisdom and will of God. In later explanations and interpretations of the original commandment God showed no leniency toward dishonor to parents. *"And he that curseth his father and mother, shall surely be put to death"* (Exod. 21:17; see Lev. 20:9). Jesus was equally adamant when he rebuked the Pharisees. *"He that speaketh evil of father or mother, let him die the death"* (Matt. 15:4). An Old Testament proverb states it starkly: *"The eye that mocketh at his father, And despiseth to obey his mother, The ravens of the valley shall pick it out, And the young eagles shall eat it"* (Prov. 30:17).

Children even as adults owe their parents honor. Timothy is instructed to teach Christians: *"But if any widow hath children or grandchildren, let them learn first to show piety towards their own family, and to requite their parents: for this is acceptable in the sight of God"* (1 Tim. 5:4).

The word *"piety"* means to *revere,* to *esteem,* to *respect,* and emanates from the *honor* one learns as a child. Children, according to Paul, who honor their fathers and mothers will *"requite"* or repay them. The context speaks of the necessities for life. Parents are to supply the needs of their offspring in childhood (2 Cor. 12:14) and children are to provide, if needed, for their parents in old age. Piety or esteem for parents demands it.

The Pharisees ignored the needs of their fathers and mothers. They gave what their parents deserved into the Jewish treasury and piously explained: *"That wherewith thou mightest have been profited by me is given to God"* (Matt. 15:5). Jesus said they dishonored their parents and were worthy of death (see Mk. 7:8-13). Anyone, Paul says, who provides not for his own — and that includes fathers and mothers — has denied the faith and is worse than an infidel (1 Tim. 5:8). Honor of parents, however, demands much beyond this.

Listen to Parents

Children have always had difficulty listening to their parents and accepting their advice. Immature youngsters cannot possibly understand the wisdom adults have gained through maturity and experience. Teenagers are influenced more by hormonal change and lust than reason. They have not walked where their parents have walked and honestly do not comprehend much of what their fathers and mothers are saying. Mark Twain stated the problem in a quaint and whimsical way: At age 14 I was appalled at my father's ignorance, but at 21 I was amazed at how much the old man had learned in just 7 years.

Children must, therefore, be trained in the impressionable years to honor their parents and trust their wisdom. That training will teach them to listen respectfully, walk by faith, and trust that what they have learned will someday make sense. Proverbs of Solomon counsel children to give heed to the wisdom of their parents.

My son, hear the instruction of thy father, And forsake not the law of thy mother (Prov. 1:8).

A wise son heareth his father's instruction; But scoffers heareth not rebuke (Prov. 13:1).

Hearken unto thy father that begat thee, And despise not thy mother when she is old (Prov. 23:22).

The story of the prodigal son is a true to life illustration of the folly of youth. What seemed good to this foolish boy before he matured proved in the grist mill of experience to be nothing more than wild oats. The blinding, glittering lights of lust and pleasure obscured what level heads of maturity could have seen plainly (see Lk. 15:11-32). Deeply rooted honor and respect would have opened the ears if not the heart of this young son.

Obey Your Parents

The child who honors his parents not only listens to them, but obeys them. Paul wrote: *"Children, obey your parents in the Lord: for this is right"* (Eph. 6:1). He also wrote, *"Children, obey your parents in all things, for this is well-pleasing in the Lord"* (Col. 3:20). Children are to obey their parents, to begin with, because *"this is right."* They are to obey their fathers and mothers also because *"this is well-pleasing in the Lord."* Obedience of children to parents is not just a nice thing. It is a sacred duty that parents must demand and children must respect. An Old Testament proverb says: *"My son, keep the commandments of thy father, And forsake not the law of thy mother"* (Prov. 6:20).

"Without natural affection," an expression that means loss of family love, and *"disobedient to parents"* were two conditions among degenerate Gentiles that qualified them in the eyes of God for death (Rom. 1:30-32). These were folks who had lost faith in the Creator, had exalted the creature to deity, refused to have God in their knowledge, had given themselves to vile passions, had sunk into a quagmire of unclean and wicked deeds, and were ruled by reprobate minds. On this long list of corruption and perversion God includes children who defiantly reject the will of their parents. They are fit only, he says, for eternal wrath (see Rom. 1:18,32; Rev. 21:8).

The obedience of children to their parents, as all other human relationships, does face one exception. As with citizens obeying civil government, wives submitting to their husbands, or employees serving their employers, children may not obey their parents in rebellion to God's law. Children obey their parent *"in the Lord"* and as *"is well-pleasing in the Lord."* God's will circumscribes all relationships. As the apostles said to the civil authorities in Jerusalem, *"We must obey God rather than men"* (Acts 5:29).

Children, for example, must never lie to obey their parents. Lying violates the moral law of God (Eph. 4:25; Rev. 21:8) — a law that supersedes parental authority. Dishonesty on behalf of the parents, immorality at the request of one's father and mother, or forsaking the assembly in submission to parental demands are not *"well-pleasing in the Lord"* (Eph. 4:25; Gal. 5:16-21; Heb. 10:25). Few children have either the courage or spiritual maturity to resist such ungodly parents. But those who do can, despite physical or verbal abuse, rest at peace — knowing that they have honored and obeyed the Highest Power in the universe. Honor and obedience to parents must never be exalted above reverence for God, and no parent should demand it.

Praise Your Parents

Parents know that children at very young ages are takers and not givers. Father and mother must provide all their needs in the early years. Children know nothing but to receive. Time and training are necessary to teach them the responsibility of giving. Here the role of parents is important. Parents who permit unbridled selfishness in the dawn of youth are spawning offspring who will lack self-denial and sacrifice at the sunset of youth.

Self-centered children develop no spirit of appreciation and receive no impressions of their parents' value. They are denied the feelings of gratitude that, again, classify them among the despicable Gentiles who, Paul says, *"neither gave thanks"* (Rom. 1:21). Children who learn nothing about thanksgiving as youths take their parents and fellow citizens for granted. Thanksgiving is an important spiritual and social value that is cultivated in children by godly parents who insist that their offspring recognize and verbalize the source of their blessings. This is the basis of praise that parents deserve, but, more importantly, that God-fearing children are trained to give. Children, of course, must first hear these things on the lips of their fathers and mothers. To add to the words of Dorothy Law Nolte (see below): "If a child lives with thanksgiving, he will learn gratitude and praise."

Children Learn What They Live With
If a child lives with criticism, he learns to condemn.
If a child lives with hostility, he learns to fight.
If a child lives with shame, he learns to feel guilty.
If a child lives with tolerance, he learns to be patient.
If a child lives with encouragement, he learns confidence.
If a child lives with fairness, he learns justice.
If a child lives with security, he learns to have faith.
If a child lives with approval, he learns to like himself.
If a child lives with acceptance and friendship, he learns to find love in the world.
Dorothy Law Nolte *via Being a Man in a Woman's World*

Consider the example and results of the worthy woman and her children. She is, first of all, a wife who loves her husband, submits to his rule, and supplies his needs. But she also is a mother who *"looketh well to the ways of her household"* (Prov. 31:27). For this dedication to her family she deserves the praise of both her husband and her children. And that she receives. *"Her children rise up and call her blessed; Her husband also, and he praiseth her"* (Prov. 31:28). Children are not by nature this thoughtful. It takes training.

How well the thoughtlessness and ingratitude of many youths are illustrated by nine of the ten lepers. Lepers were outcasts who could neither live in society nor in their homes. They could not kiss their wives, hug their children, or experience any of the joys of family life. And yet when they were healed of their leprosy by Jesus and enabled to return to a normal life, they gave no thanks or glory to the Lord. One of them, though, *"turned back, with a loud voice glorifying God; and he fell upon his face at his feet, giving him thanks"* (Lk. 17:15,16).

The apostle Paul teaches Christians that their prayers, supplications, and requests should be made to God with thanksgiving (Phil. 4:6). God-fearing parents are alert to nurture this spirit in their children. A child who knows to petition his parents for his needs must likewise learn to thank them and praise them when that need is supplied.

A grave injustice is done to children when they grow up with no recognition of who changed their diapers and wiped their snotty noses, who paced the floors and rocked them when they were in pain, and who bathed and fed them when they were helpless. It is likewise unfair for children to live in ignorance of the sacrifices that were made to provide their food, shelter, and clothing. Parents who are concerned to train their children in the nurture and admonition of the Lord must not forget the important elements of "thanksgiving" and "praise." Children need not be middle-aged before they rise up and call their fathers and mothers *"blessed."* They can learn this from their youth up!

Value of Discipline

The word "discipline" comes from the same root as the word "disciple" and means "to learn." It is more narrowly used today to refer to punishment or chastisement that parents administer to disobedient children. What must be remembered about the original meaning of the word "discipline" and its more limited use today is that punishment is a form of teaching. Both parents and children must understand its value. No child should grow up thinking his parents are mean and unfair.

A small child who carelessly runs out in the street needs a strong lesson for his protection. A youngster who refuses to perform his chores must be severely taught that responsibility is a vital part of life. A kid who smart-mouths his parents or resists their authority will not learn otherwise without the purifying element of pain. But what is essential in all acts of discipline is the presence of love. Children, as is now more and more common, are not to be beaten and abused. Children must sense no spirit of malice and hatred. When chastening proceeds out of love, it teaches children *"reverence"* for their parents (see Heb. 12:5-9). Several proverbs underscore the importance and value of discipline:

A fool despiseth his father's correction; but he that regardeth reproof getteth prudence (Prov. 15:5).

The rod and reproof give wisdom; but a child left to himself causeth shame to his mother (Prov. 29:15).

Correct thy son, and he will give thee rest; Yea, he will give delight unto thy soul (Prov. 29:17).

Conclusion

If children are to honor their fathers and mothers, listen to them, obey them, praise them, and profit from their discipline, they must be taught to *"remember also thy Creator in the days of thy youth"* (Eccl. 12:1).

Today's youth are bombarded almost daily with the evolutionary and humanistic concept that man is a product of animals. The number one truth, then, that parents must drive home to their children is the understanding of their origin. Children must know without doubt that they are a product of God; that they are made in the image of God and cannot live by bread alone. Parents must not let them forget for one day that within those fleshly bodies dwells an eternal spirit that must live by every word that proceedeth out of the mouth of God (see Gen. 1:26,27; Matt. 4:4).

When this fact is drilled into children, they will mature with the knowledge that man must not live like animals in slavery to fleshly lusts. The youth of today need to learn by self-control to bring their carnal appetites into subjection to their spirits (see Matt. 26:40,41; 1 Cor. 9:24-27) and their spirits into submission to God's Spirit (see Rom. 8:12-17; Gal. 5:16-23).

Young people can sow to the flesh or the Spirit. But they must be reminded often: when they sow to the flesh, they will of the flesh reap corruption — eternal damnation, punishment, and destruction from the face of God; when they sow to the Spirit, they will of the Spirit reap everlasting life (see Gal. 6:7,8; 2 Thess. 1:7-9).

Children who are trained unceasingly from youth to know and remember their Creator will honor both God and their parents *"that it may be well with thee"* (Eph. 6:3).

An Outline Study Guide

Introduction:

A. What view should parents take concerning sassing and acts of disrespect?_

_____

B. Should children be heard? _____

What is the correct way for them to be heard? _____

_____

C. Discuss the Dobson quotation about the call to battle and seek "pros" and "cons." State your view._____

_____

I. Honor Thy Parents:

A. What did Moses say about this (Ex. 20:12)?_____

_____

Where is it repeated in the New Testament?_____

Define the word "honor": _____

_____

B. How seriously did Jehovah take this (Ex. 21:17; Lev. 20:9)?_____

_____

What did Jesus say about it (Matt. 15:4)?_____

_____

How did Proverbs 30:17 put it? _____

_____

C. How are children as adults to honor their parents (1 Tim. 5:4)?_____

_____

How does Paul classify those who don't (1 Tim. 5:8)? _____

_____

How did Pharisees get around this (Mk. 7:8-13)? _____

_____

II. Listen To Parents:

A. Why do children have difficulty understanding the wisdom of their parents?

_____

How did Mark Twain put it? _____

_____

B. Summarize what Proverbs 1:8; 13:1; 23:22 say: _____

_____

How does the prodigal son illustrate the folly of youth (Lk. 15:11-32)?_

_____

III. Obey Your Parents:

A. What two reasons are given for children to obey parents (Eph. 6:1; Col. 3:20)?

_____

How did Solomon put it (Prov. 6:20)? _____

_____

B. How did degenerate Gentiles feel about obedience to parents (Rom. 1:30,31)?

_____

How does God feel about this disrespect (Rom. 1:18,32)?_____

_____

C. Is there any exception to children obeying parents (Acts 5:29)? _____

_____

Cite examples._____

_____

IV. Praise Your Parents:

A. What will parents receive from children who are thankful (Prov. 31:27,28)?

_____

How will children learn to be thankful?_____

_____

B. What value does gratitude have for them as Christians (Lk. 17:11-19; Phil. 4:6)? _____

_____

V. Value of Discipline:
A. What is the origin of the word "discipline" and what does it mean?___

_____

How does this meaning relate to punishment? _____

_____

B. What must always accompany discipline (Heb. 12:6)?_____

_____

What are some things children should be punished for?_____

_____

C. Cite several Proverbs that teach on the subject of discipline: _____

_____

Conclusion:
A. What must children be taught to assure they will honor their parents (Eccl. 12:1)?

_____

In whose image were they made (Gen. 1:26)? _____

_____

B. By what must children live (Matt. 4:4)? _____

_____

What happens when they sow to the flesh (Gal. 6:7,8)? _____

_____

To the Spirit? _____

_____

C. What must children be taught about fleshly lusts (1 Cor. 9:24-27; 1 John 2:15,16; Gal. 5:16-23)? _____

_____

Working Parents

Introduction

The times when dad and mom and the kids lived together as a working unit down on the farms are gone forever. Times were simpler then: no husbands taking female business associates to lunch or sitting behind closed doors with secretaries on their laps; no wives rushing madly to babysitters and on to work; no kids running the streets with the few derelicts of society; no TV to fill the minds of the parents and the kids with greed, lust, and the ills of society; no scattering of the family to the four winds every evening. Families were closer in those days: working and eating meals together; visiting, laughing, and playing games together; reading the Bible, praying, and discussing right and wrong together. Spiritually, these were the best of opportunities.

Families may mourn the passing of the "good old days" and fret over the loss of valuable assets that went with them, but no amount of nostalgia can re-establish the former times. Those times, of course, had their own set of problems and only dreamers portray them as a fairy tale existence. Few families today, now that they have seen "Paree," could be hogtied and dragged back to the old homesteads. Reality beckons parents and children to the 21st century and principles call them to arm for the battle against a stronghold of modern challenges and problems.

One of those challenging problems arose with a drastic change in society and family life following World War II. At first a trickle of wives and mothers made their way into the work force — more out of necessity than desire. Ere long, a taste for things money can buy was developed and the faint flow of women into the job market became a steady stream. The psychology of wanting the children to have more than the depression gave them took deep root and parents began to buy things rather than give love. Add to this the rise of the female ego and the competitive spirit of the feminist movement and the stage is set for the challenge of a "motherless society."

This problem is paralleled by the working father who, after long days at the office or plant, has all but turned the reins of the household over to the mother. After all, he reasons, she stays home all day and doesn't have to work; it's only fair that she take care of the kids in the evening while *"I"* relax and catch *"my"* breath. The family, therefore, is either "motherless" or "fatherless" and often both. An easy solution to the problem is to leave the education of the children to the church, the schools, TV, and their friends. Both parents in many homes are dominated by their work and careers, have opted out of their roles in the family, and have left the kids to find their own way.

Please, fathers and mothers who are Christians, do not skip this chapter, thinking this is only a problem for worldly and secularistic families. Christians today, as ancient Israel in Canaan, are influenced by the nations around them and are in great numbers bowing before the god of materialism, as surely as Israel built altars to Baal. Some hard decisions face working dads and moms who are Christians if they are to set their minds on things above (Col. 3:1,2), seek the kingdom of God first (Matt. 6:33), and nurture their children in the chastening and admonition of the Lord (Eph. 6:4).

Fathers — Honor of Work

America was settled mainly by European stock who grew up under the capitalism and work ethic that came out of the Renaissance and Reformation. The pioneer spirit and hard work among these settlers are well known, and the economic greatness of this country flourished because this spirit survived through each generation unto the present. And who can find fault with this? Not even Christians deny the honorableness of hard work.

Work can be traced to Eden when man was commanded by God to *"dress"* and *"keep"* the garden (Gen. 2:15). Jehovah also cursed the ground after man sinned and ordered him that by *"the sweat of thy face shalt thou eat bread"* (Gen. 3:19; 5:29). When the church at Thessalonica encountered problems with a brother who refused to work, who sponged off of the brethren and became a busybody, Paul wrote: *"If any will not work, neither let him eat"* (2 Thess. 3:10). The apostle also told them *"that with quietness they work, and eat their own bread"* (3:12) and that they *"have no company"* with a brother who refuses to work (3:14).

Paul, using a military term, described the lazy brother as *"disorderly"* (2 Thess. 3:6). A brother who will not work is a soldier out of step with God's commandments and insubordinate to divine orders. This is the same apostle who used the term "unbeliever" or "infidel" to denote a man who neglects to provide for his family (1 Tim. 5:4,8). He also says a man should *"labor, working with his hands"* to supply the needs of anyone who cannot provide for himself (Eph. 4:28). And those who work are to do it with honesty and dedication, serving their employers in singleness of heart as though they were working for the Lord (Eph. 6:5-8).

Fathers — Abuse of Work

Although work is honorable, it may not be assumed that "more work" is more honorable. Work, as any good thing, can be abused. When a good thing is exalted to the neglect of other good things, sin and corruption result. No one, for example, denies the need for leisure or relaxation. But what happens when ease — whether in fishing, golf, or hobbies — interferes with the duty to assemble with the saints? A good thing is abused and sin results (see Heb. 10:25). This also happens with work. Consider several examples.

Fathers, now that the work force is filled with women, face the problem of *"silly women laden with sins"* and are often taken captive and *"led away by divers lusts"* (2 Tim. 3:6). Who can doubt that the rise in adultery among fathers results from men spending time on coffee breaks, at lunch, and on the job "innocently" socializing with women. An employee, Paul says, is to give himself with singleness of heart to the work of his employer (see Eph. 6:5-8). Fathers who divert themselves from work and from the role as breadwinners for companionship with females are being drawn into a common temptation that threatens family life.

Fathers also encounter the problem of greed. Christians are to be content with the necessities of life (1 Tim. 6:8). Fathers who are *"minded to be rich"* fall into temptations, snares, and a host of hurtful lusts. *"Love of money"* is a root of all kinds of evil that many fathers reach after and fall from the faith, piercing themselves through with many sorrows (1 Tim. 6:9-11). Working fathers must honestly challenge the grip of greed that now controls American workers — including Christians. It is an abuse of his role to work needless hours in neglect of his family for the mere sake of promotions or the accumulation of more mammon (see Matt. 6:19,20). Covetousness, the lust for more, is idolatry, a god whom many bread-winners worship and adore more than their families (Col. 3:5; Eph. 5:5).

Work And Neglect Of Family

We have deluded ourselves into believing that circumstances have forced us to work too hard for a short time, when, in fact, we are driven from *within*. We lack the discipline to limit our entanglements with the world, choosing instead to be dominated by our work and the materialistic gadgetry it will bring. And what is sacrificed in the process are the loving relationships with wives and children and friends who give life meaning (p. 139).

— **James C. Dobson**, *Straight Talk to Men and Their Wives*

Finally, fathers abuse work when it is used to divert their roles to mothers. God squarely placed on the shoulders of fathers the duty to rule the household and nurture the children in the chastening and admonition of the Lord (1 Tim. 3:4; Eph. 6:4). Fathers must not ignore this responsibility. They must take charge: see that the TV is turned off, that the family is gathered each night for prayer, Bible study and communication, and that the home is restored as a unit. They must not — yes, *"must not"* — allocate this role to mothers to perform while they are at work.

Mothers — Honor of Work

Work also is honorable for women. The "worthy woman" was commended for working willingly with her hands, bringing her bread from afar, considering a field and buying it, planting a vineyard with the fruit of her hands, spinning yarn, sewing carpets and garments, and selling to merchants (see Prov. 31:13-24). Women in biblical times also drew water, tended sheep, gleaned fields, and beat out grain (see Gen. 24:16; 29:6,9; Ruth 2:17; John 4:7). Lydia, a business woman of Thyatira, was at Philippi selling purple and Priscilla, a faithful wife, may have worked with her husband in the tentmaking business (Acts 16:14; 18:1-3).

Scripture, it is evident, does not outright condemn women for working — even outside the home. This is not to say the practice is right under all circumstances and is without danger or sin. Other factors have to be considered to answer the vital and gnawing question of when women sin by entering the public work force. The problem is often complicated and can only be answered truthfully by husbands and wives who receive God's word with "honest" and "good" hearts (see Lk. 8:15).

Mothers — Abuse of Work

That work is honorable for women is not scriptural license for mothers to leave the home to work merely to pursue dollars. The contexts of the biblical examples above do not bear out why these women worked these jobs or that in their work they left the home. It is, then, necessary to examine why women work outside the home and whether that work hinders their duties as wives, mothers, and Christians.

First, as in the case of fathers, mothers who work outside the home must avoid becoming *"silly women laden with sins"* who are *"led away by divers lusts"* (2 Tim. 3:6). Women who create close bonds of friendship with male employees are setting a trap for themselves. When neglected at home, they are often enticed to pour out their feelings to a compassionate man unto whom they then become prey for emotional attachment and affection. Mothers who enter public work need to remember that they are also to serve their employer in a singleness of heart as unto the Lord. They are not there to court the favor of men — men who may have ungodliness on their minds.

Second, boredom is no excuse for mothers to leave the home in search of employment. Many mothers offer this reason, especially the ones whose children are in school or gone from the nest. God-fearing women should never be bored with life. Time is needed for daily Bible study to grow in the Lord, to prepare oneself to teach youngsters, and to teach younger women to be good Christians, wives, and mothers (see Heb. 5:11-14; Tit. 2:3-5).

Visiting the sick or elderly, participating in women's Bible classes, preparing meals for the bereaved, conducting home studies for neighbors and friends, doing important volunteer work are of far more worth than extra cash in the bank. And what about babysitting for younger mothers while they shop, visit the sick, or spend an evening alone with their husbands? Remember Dorcas, Phoebe, and Priscilla (Acts 9:36-39; Rom. 16:1-3; Acts 18:24-28)? Boredom is a poor excuse for mothers who are Christians to enter all the temptations, entanglements, pressures, and problems of the working world.

Third, it is disturbing to hear women speak of leaving the home to work because the kids drive them up a wall. Mothers who do not love their children, relish the responsibility of training them, and enjoy the role of homemakers are, as Christians, rejecting God (see Tit. 2:4,5; Prov. 1:8; 6:20; 1 Tim. 5:14). Some have soothed the conscience by farming the kids out to day-care centers under the guise that it enhances children's social development. What a cop out!

Fourth, careers frequently get in the way of motherhood. Many woman nowadays earn college degrees and establish careers before they marry. When they marry and have children it is difficult for them to "waste" all that education to be "just a housewife." Not a few — even Christians — are influenced by the feminist movement, have development inflated egos, and want to compete with men. Many have proved their prowess in the business world and once they have, it is just too ordinary, too degrading, and too demeaning to lower themselves to the fashionable form of slavery that is falsely attached to housewivery. That Christians could think this way is unthinkable — totally at odds with the value system God revealed in Scriptures. Mothers who reason this way need to read again Proverbs 31, where the "worthy woman" is a mother and housewife. She is priceless, the Lord says, and her value is far above rubies.

Fifth, women often work outside the home because of family greed. Many husbands insist that their wives work so the family can have a nicer home, a better car, the finest furniture and drapes, designer clothes, a VCR, the most expensive golf clubs or fishing equipment, membership in country clubs, power saws and drills and other tools, and who knows what else. Families — again, Christians included — are undoubtedly influenced by the god of materialism that controls the neighbors, fellow workers, and some affluent brethren. The Joneses still have much to say about what folks feel they must have.

Family Neglect

The paramount issue in solving the problems of working parents is — priorities. Fathers have to tackle the difficulty of whether long hours, more money, higher positions will take precedent over the needs of their wives and children. When the wife's needs for companionship, sexual and emotional fulfillment, love and appreciation are not met because of work, the husband's role as God designed it has not been performed. When the children's need for attention, affection, teaching, discipline, and admiration are ignored day after day because dad is too busy, the father's role has been put on the back burner. When lust for money or power drives the husband and father to work, work, work, he is blind to what's really important in life. Work is honorable and necessary, but it is a dishonor to Christians when they unnecessarily neglect their families and use it to attain purely carnal goals (see Matt. 6:33; Col. 3:1,2).

Wives and mothers who reject their chief role as workers at home and managers of the household are not only neglecting their husbands and children, but are rejecting Christ their Master who assigned those roles. No one can deny that in some instances women need to work outside the home, but when it results from boredom, lust for careers, or greed, it is a folly that will inevitably bear evil fruit.

Wives and mothers, as seen in the previous lesson, were designed suitably to help their husbands and the fathers of their children in the home (Gen. 2:18-20). When as a result of public work, they are too busy or too tired to prepare a warm meal for the family, to be affectionate and attentive to their husbands and children, and to serve their unique and important role in the home, a vital bond that cements and unites the household is missing. Women are gradually acknowledging that "super moms" do not exist, that when they work outside the home something has to be sacrificed. Guess what is it? The rationalization that "quality" time with the husbands and the kids is sufficient reveals that "quantity" time is given to herself and her career. To reverse this, she admits, would destroy her career, but as it stands now she sees no serious threat to the home. What convoluted logic! What deception!

Conclusion

Families, it is certain, cannot go back to the "good old days." But the bond and unity of yesterday's households must be preserved. Togetherness is important, Bible-centered training is a must, and the roles of both father and mother are necessary. The urban, work-oriented, greed-dominated society of modern America cannot be allowed to interfere with what God ordained the home to be. When it does — even among Christians — the family is setting itself up for indifference, alienation, dissatisfaction, and, for what all too often is happening, divorce. Brethren, these things must not be!

An Outline Study Guide

Introduction:

A. What existed in the "good old days" in families that needs to be restored?_

_____

B. What developed after World War II that disrupted family life? _____

_____

What parallel problem developed among fathers? _____

_____

How have these twin problems affected the home?_____

_____

C. What must be the priorities of Christians (Col. 3:1,2; Matt. 6:33)?_____

_____

I. Fathers — Honor of Work:

A. What does Paul say about a man who will not work (2 Thess. 3:10)?_

_____

How is this man to be treated (2 Thess. 3:12,14)? _____

_____

B. What does Paul mean by disorderly (2 Thess. 3:6)? _____

_____

For what two reasons should man work (1 Tim. 5:4,8; Eph. 4:28)?___

_____

C. What is the proper attitude toward an employer (Eph. 6:5-8)?_____

_____

II. Fathers — Abuse of Work:

A. What are two major problems fathers now face in the work force (2 Tim. 3:6; 1 Tim. 6: 8-11)? _____

_____

B. What should not be the goal of work (Matt. 6:19,20)?_____

_____

How does Paul characterize covetousness (Col. 3:5; Eph. 5:5)?_____

_____

C. What role do fathers have in the home (1 Tim. 3:4; Eph. 6:4)?_____

_____

Suggest ways they can take charge._____

_____

III. Mothers — Honor of Work:
  A. What does the "worthy" woman reveal about the honor of work among mothers (Prov. 31:13-24)?_____

    _____

  B. List and discuss other women and their work (Gen. 24:6; 29:6,9; Ruth 2:17; John 4:7; Acts 16:14; Acts 18:1-3)._____

    _____

  C. Is it always a sin for a woman to work outside the home? _____

    _____

    Justify your answer. _____

    _____

    How can a father and mother determine when it is sinful (Lk. 8:15)?___

    _____

IV. Mothers — Abuse of Work:
  A. Why must women who work in public be wary of male relationships (2 Tim. 3:6)? _____

    How can problems develop?_____

    _____

  B. Discuss boredom as a reason to work outside the home (Heb. 5:11-14; Tit. 2:3-5; Acts 9:36-39; Rom. 16:1-3; Acts 18:24-28)._____

    _____

  C. Assess mothers who work because their kids drive them up the wall (Tit. 2:4,5; Prov. 1:8; 6:20; 1 Tim. 5:14). _____

    Discuss the "pros" and "cons" of day care centers. _____

    _____

  D. How would you compare "career" versus "homemaker."_____

    _____

V. Family Neglect:
  A. How would you relate the problems of work with priorities (Col. 3:1,2; Matt. 6:33)?_____

    _____

  B. Spend some time discussing the "pros" and "cons" of "quality time" versus "quantity time."_____

    _____

Conclusions:
A. What are some assets of the "good old days" that could be practiced today?

_____

B. What must not be allowed to dominate the home today?_____

_____

What are some results when it does?_____

_____

What God Hath Joined Together

Introduction

Security in marriage nowadays is a fragile item. Couples have little more than a 50/50 chance that their relationship will survive. Between 30 and 40 percent of marriages now end in divorce. Among teenagers the figure is closer to 50 percent. That this is tragic, shameful, and outrageous is acknowledged by all sane and responsible people. But fewer and fewer folks are willing to forego the lusts and deviant behavior that fuel this problem. Modern society is dominated by a "me philosophy" that grants no quarter to anything that interferes with what "I want." And if "my wants" happen to step on the rights of "my" mate or demand taking someone else's companion — so be it.

Welcome to a "Christian" nation that knows not Christ, is devoid of the spirit of Christ, and rejects the teaching of Christ on this vital topic. Is there anything that can be done, brethren? Moaning, groaning, handwringing, and spouting statistics certainly won't slow the escalating divorce rate. That the Lord's church can have much national impact on the breakdown of marriage is unlikely. But what it surely can and must do is set its own house in order. Divorce is growing at an alarming rate among brethren and something must be done — right now! The teaching of Christ on divorce and remarriage must be inculcated into the minds of brethren and their children and the fearful consequences of disobedience must be assimilated into their consciences. The next two lessons are designed to offer some help in reaching these goals.

This country, of course, is not the first nation to face the disgraceful scandal of divorce. It created difficulties for Moses among the Jews of his time and it was a pervasive problem in the Roman Empire at the time of Christ and the apostles. The Lord, however, refused to circumvent the issue or to soften his view to appease the masses. Jesus was forthright, unequivocal, and demanding.

John the Baptist, the staunch pioneer of the Lord, broke ground on this subject along with many other topics when he sought to prepare the way for the coming Messiah. His work was to make ready a people for the Lord (Lk. 1:17). Preparation for the Messianic kingdom demanded confession of sins, repentance, and baptism. John took a hard line, boldly commanding the people to renounce and forsake sin. He minced no words and spared no one in his strong protest against unrighteous living. Soldiers and publicans were among the multitudes who found themselves in the path of John's withering blasts (see Lk. 3:1-14).

But the most celebrated example of John's denunciation of sin was Herod the tetrarch (Matt. 14:1-12). Herod had married his brother's wife and was living with her in adultery. John condemned him to his face. *"It is not lawful for thee to have her"* (Matt. 14:4). Herodias, Herod's adulteress wife, was angered by this brash wilderness prophet. She manipulated a prison sentence for John and then engineered his death.

The case of Herod and Herodias illustrates the problem that confronts families today. Men and women without hesitation take to themselves wives and husbands who in God's eyes are bound to other mates. Citizens of this land are imprisoned for stealing a neighbor's automobile, electrocuted for taking his life, but face no civil recourse for marrying his wife. But what is more disturbing is that these adulterers and adulteresses receive not so much as a rebuke from many Christians and most religious denominations.

When John rebuked sinners and ordered them to repent, he left no doubt about what that demanded. *"Bring forth fruits worthy of repentance"* was his cry (Lk. 3:8). Publicans asked him what that meant. He told them to quit cheating people. *"Extort no more than that which is appointed you"* (Lk. 3:13). When soldiers asked how it applied to them, he told them to cease wrongfully accusing people and defrauding them by violence (Lk. 3:14). Repentance is no less rigid for man today — even in the case of those who have another's companion.

Brethren must not shrink back from declaring the whole counsel of God (Acts 20:27), including what the Lord says about divorce and remarriage. Couples who find themselves with mates who belong to another need to know what the Lord's will is and what repentance and obedience demand. This first lesson will analyze passages that teach the permanence of marriage. A second lesson will seek to answer objections to that analysis. Companions and prospective companions must be taught: *"What therefore God hath joined together, let not man put asunder"* (Matt. 19:6).

Matthew 5:31,32

The most notable of Jesus' sermons contains a contrast between his teaching on divorce and the permissive regulations allowed by Moses. The Lord taught: *"It was said also, Whosoever shall put away his wife, let him give her a writing of divorcement: but I say unto you, that everyone that putteth away his wife, saving for the cause of fornication, maketh her an adulteress: and whoever shall marry her when she is put away committeth adultery"* (Matt. 5:31,32).

Moses had granted bills of divorce and the right to put away one's mate for many causes (see Matt. 19:3,7), but Jesus says no to this. The Lord grants approval for divorce only if one's partner is guilty of fornication. The term "fornication," unlike its limited use today of cohabitation by unmarried couples, meant "illicit sexual intercourse in general" (Thayer). It even included homosexuality (Jude 7). Jesus uses it of sexual relations between spouses and someone other than their husband or wife.

When sexual infidelity has not occurred, Jesus permits no divorce or remarriage. Companions who divorce for reasons other than fornication and remarry enter an illicit relationship. The expression *"committeth adultery"* is present tense and, according to Greek scholars, indicates continual action or practice. Each instance of sexual union in an unlawful marriage would, accordingly, be an act of adultery. As John the Baptist said: *"It is not lawful for thee to have her."*

Matthew 19:3-9

The question Jesus discussed in the sermon on the mount (Matt. 5:31,32) was raised later by the Pharisees to test him. They often took hard questions that stumped or divided the rabbis and put them to Jesus to see how he would respond. This time they asked: *"Is it lawful for a man to put away his wife for every cause?"* Some rabbis, based on Deuteronomy 24:1-4, had said yes. Jesus admits that this was permitted by Moses because of the stubbornness and hardness of Israel's heart (v. 8), but challenges its legitimacy in God's sight.

Jesus reaches back beyond Moses' day in search of God's answer to this question. At the beginning, man was to *"leave"* his father and mother, *"cleave"* unto his wife, and the two *"shall become one flesh"* (see Gen. 2:24). After stating that, Jesus declared: *"What therefore God hath joined together, let not man put asunder"* (v. 6). Moses, the Lord explains, may have allowed divorce for every cause at the demands of Israel, *"but from the beginning it hath not been so"* (v. 8).

Jesus with that background now answers the question. *"And I say unto you, Whosoever shall put away his wife, except for fornication, and shall marry another, committeth adultery: and he that marrieth her when she is put away committeth adultery"* (v. 9). A couple of ideas are obvious in this answer. First, Jesus is restating God's intentions from the beginning, and, second, God's law antedates Moses and applies to all men — *"whosoever."*

Jesus replies to both parties in a divorce. The partner who puts away his companion, *"except for fornication,"* and marries another commits adultery. The relationship is illicit. The mate who is put away cannot remarry without committing adultery. It is an unlawful marriage. Jesus is clear on this point for both parties. The only legitimate basis for divorce and remarriage is fornication — "illicit sexual intercourse" (Thayer).

Mark 10:11,12 and Luke 16:18

Mark's and Luke's accounts of Jesus' teaching do not mention the exception. This does not eliminate it, but focuses on divorce and remarriage for every cause. Mark writes: *"And he saith unto them, Whosoever shall put away his wife, and marry another, committeth adultery against her: and if she herself shall put away her husband, and marry another, she committeth adultery."* Luke says: *"Every one that putteth away his wife, and marrieth another, committeth adultery: and he that marrieth one that is put away from a husband committeth adultery."* Mark, unlike the other gospels, shows that marriage regulations apply also to wives putting away their husbands. Luke, as the two passages in Matthew, notes that a third party who marries a divorcee also commits adultery.

Evidently a situation similar to circumstances in this country prevailed then. Men or women put away their partners for any cause and remarried. Jesus took his stand against it. Jesus sought to re-establish marriage as God designed it. It was a permanent relationship at the beginning and must be today. Husbands and wives who put away their companions for every cause and remarry commit adultery. Why this is so becomes obvious in two passages from the epistles.

Romans 7:2,3

The apostle Paul touched on marriage when illustrating the relationship of Jews to Moses' law after Christ came. *"For the woman that hath a husband is bound by the law to the husband while he liveth; but if the husband die, she is discharged from the law of the husband. So then if, while the husband liveth, she be joined to another man, she shall be called an adulteress: but if the husband die, she is free from the law, so that she is no adulteress, though she be joined to another man."*

First, Paul states the permanency of marriage. A wife is bound to her husband as long as he lives. The word "bound" means "to bind, to tie." The two are tied together. If civil law releases partners when divorce is granted, then Paul must be speaking from some other point of view. When he says companions are tied together till death, he certainly does not state Roman or Jewish law. Paul reveals God's law. It is God who binds husbands and wives together until death. Paul, for contextual reasons, states God's law without the exception given by Jesus. The fact that it had no bearing on Paul's immediate point and is not included here does not eliminate its validity.

Second, since God binds husbands and wives together till death, neither partner can be *"joined"* to another while the other is alive. A woman who becomes wife to a "different" (Greek) man while her husband lives is called an *"adulteress."* Civil law has no bearing on what Paul is saying and cannot change his conclusions by granting a divorce. God, regardless of civil law, binds a woman to her husband while he lives. To be *"joined"* at that time to a different man is immoral.

Third, if the husband dies, the woman is *"free"* from God's law that binds the two. She is no longer tied to her husband. She may now *"be joined to another man"* and in so doing *"she is no adulteress."* The essential point in all this is: even civil law cannot put asunder what God has joined together and cannot make pure what God calls adultery.

1 Corinthians 7:10-16

The apostle Paul, in what has become a rather controversial Scripture, adds several important thoughts to the Lord's teaching on marriage. Some of what he says concerned a *"present distress"* and has no bearing on the permanency of marriage. A few ideas, though, relate directly to divorce and remarriage. An example: *"But unto the married I give charge, yea not I, but the Lord, that the wife depart not from her husband"* (v. 10).

Paul delivers this as a *"charge"* from the Lord. It is an order or command. The Lord insists that a wife is not to *"depart"* from her husband. The word *"depart"* is the same word translated *"put asunder"* in Matthew 19:6. A wife is not to leave, break off the relationship with, or separate from the man to whom God *"joined"* and *"bound"* her.

Paul next supposes that some Christians might violate this injunction. If they do depart from their mate, what options are then open to them? *"But should she depart, let her remain unmarried, or else be reconciled to her husband; and that the husband leave not the wife"* (v. 11). The wife who *"departs"* from her husband, Paul says, must not compound her sin by marrying another. She may only, if she departs, remain single or be reunited to her husband.

But what if a husband or wife is married to an unbeliever? Is the relationship legitimate and should they continue to dwell together? Is this reason for divorce? To the husband in these circumstances, Paul said, *"Let him not leave her"* (v. 12). To the wife: *"Let her not leave her husband"* (v. 13). Why? *"For the unbelieving husband is sanctified in the wife, and the unbelieving wife is sanctified in the brother"* (v. 14). The relationship, as the word *"sanctified"* means, is holy and is to be preserved.

The unbeliever, though, not bound in conscience by God's law, may decide to leave. What then? *"Let him depart: the brother or sister is not under bondage in such cases: but God hath called us to peace"* (v. 15). The term *"bondage"* has spawned considerable theorizing and given birth to views not stated by Paul. An example: Since the Christian is not under bondage in this instance, he is free to remarry. Paul neither says nor implies this.

The argument is based on what Paul affirms later in the chapter. He states that a wife is not "bound" to her husband after his death and is free to remarry (v. 39). Accordingly, some contend that a Christian who is not *"under bondage"* to an unbeliever is free to remarry. The view assumes that *"bondage"* is the same as *"bound."* The word *"bound"* (v. 39) is the term used in Romans 7:2 and denotes the spiritual bond that God creates when he ties or joins a husband and wife in marriage. The word *"bondage"* (v. 15) is a form of the term "bondservant" and describes a companion's responsibility to serve the needs of his mate.

When unbelieving partners depart, they forfeit their rights to the benefits of marriage. Believers are no longer responsible for their needs. A wife's obligations, for example, to the unbeliever's physical, sexual, emotional, social, spiritual demands cease. She is free from her duties as a wife. Believing mates, in cases when unbelievers depart, have always, as the perfect tense indicates, been free from their role to serve. Nothing, however, is said about the right to be joined to another. The options outlined earlier in the chapter would apply: she must remain unmarried or be reconciled to her husband (v. 11). Nothing except fornication on the husband's part can change that (see Matt. 5:32; 19:9).

As one might suppose, many objections to the ideas in this lesson have been raised. The intention here has been to set forth plainly what these verses teach. Another lesson will be necessary to study these objections.

An Outline Study Guide
Introduction:
A. What is the main philosophy behind divorce?_____

_____

B. What did John the Baptist demand that people do about sin (Matt. 3:5-8)?_

_____

   What did he tell publicans and soldiers to do (Lk. 3:13,14)?_____

_____

C. What did he say to Herod about his marriage (Matt. 14:4)?_____

_____

I. Matthew 5:31,32:

A. What did Moses grant the people?_____

_____

For what cause did Jesus grant divorce?_____

_____

B. Define "fornication": _____

_____

How general is its meaning (Jude 7)?_____

_____

C. What results if one divorces for reasons other than fornication and remarries?

_____

What does the present tense of the word "committeth" imply?_____

_____

II. Matthew 19:3-9:

A. Why did Moses so readily permit divorce?_____

_____

B. To what does Jesus appeal in answering the Pharisees' question (vv. 4,5,8; Gen. 2:24)? _____

_____

C. What conclusion does Jesus reach (v. 6)?_____

_____

What exception does he give (v. 9)?_____

_____

III. Mark 10:11,12 and Luke 16:18:

A. In view of differences in "great commission" accounts (Matt. 28:18-20; Mk. 16:15,16; Lk. 24:45-47), does Mark and Luke's elimination of the exception annul its validity? _____

_____

B. What does Mark include that other accounts do not?_____

_____

What does Luke discuss that Mark doesn't?_____

_____

Since the exception phrase is not included, what is the focus of these two accounts? _____

_____

IV. Romans 7:2,3:

A. What is said here about the permanency of marriage?_____

What does "bound" mean? _____

_____

B. What happens to a wife who is joined to a "different" man while her husband lives? _____

_____

What is her situation if her husband dies?_____

_____

C. What bearing does civil law have on these conclusions? Can it free where God does not? _____

_____

V. 1 Corinthians 7:10-16:
A. What is a wife forbidden to do (v. 10)?_____

_____

If she does depart, what are her options (v. 11)?_____

_____

B. How does Paul characterize marriage to an unbeliever (vv. 12,13)?_____

_____

If the unbeliever deserts, what is the obligation of the believer (v. 15)?_

_____

C. What does "not under bondage" mean? _____

_____

Does it mean the same as "not bound" in verse 39? _____

_____

D. A Christian can only divorce and remarry if what is involved on the part of the unbeliever (Matt. 5:31,32; 19:9)?_____

_____

Committeth Adultery

Introduction

Sin comes easy and is often fun, but its consequences are hard and costly — sometimes deadly. A drinking party at a nearby university was lots of laughs last week, but this week the funeral is being conducted for the winner — the young man who drank the most. And what is worse, the lad must still face his Creator in judgment (see Gal. 5:19-21; 1 Cor. 6:9-11). Office romances are exciting, the adultery and marriage that result seem so right, and compassion for their jilted spouses is lost in the euphoria of new found "love." But when the mist of romance lifts and clouds of reality obscure the stars before the eyes of the newlyweds, the guilty couple who were unfaithful to their mates and had no grounds for divorce face the state of their relationship before God. What must they do?

The scenario of divorce is not always that blatant. What about the couple who is selfish, inconsiderate, immature, and irresponsible? He cares nothing for her needs, spends his time in pleasure, thoughtlessly ignores his role in the marriage, and provides no romance or emotional support for his wife. She sits at home reading trashy magazines and filling her mind with the garbage of soap operas, runs around spending them into the poorhouse, and mindlessly neglects her duties as a wife. The two wake up one morning to the reality that no personal bond exists between them, decide that they do not even like one another, and without biblical grounds head for the divorce court. A few months later they find themselves in "love" with someone else, remarry, and forget forever the vows and contract they made with God and one another. Again, what must they do?

The plot thickens when children are born into these kinds of relationships. The couple decides they need to "go to church" for the sake of the kids. They talk to the preacher or elders about "joining" the church. Their previous marriages and unscriptural reasons for divorce come to light. What should they be told? This is no far out hypothetical situation, brethren; it is a circumstance that personal workers face about every third call they make these days.

Compassion and common sense say to teach them the gospel, explain God's forgiveness, and ignore their marital state. Truth, however, does not emanate from sympathy and human wisdom. How a teacher of God feels and what he personally thinks is not God's standard of judgment (Jn. 12:48). Only truth can free a man from sin, only truth can save sinners from God's wrath, only truth can sanctify a crooked and perverse people — and that truth is God's word (Jn. 8:32; Eph. 1:13,14: Jn.

17:17; 1 Pet. 1:22,23). It is that word, that truth, that must be taught!

The cost of discipleship has always been high and servants of the Master in modern times must not seek to make a "cheap sale." Jesus said, *"So therefore whosoever he be of you that renounceth not all that he hath, he cannot be my disciple"* (Lk. 14:33). The Lord said earlier in this text that following him demands denying father, mother, children, brothers, sisters, and one's own life (vv. 26,27). On another occasion Jesus told a man to sell all his goods and feed the poor if he wanted to go to heaven (Matt. 19:16-22). Even when Jesus was compassionate toward sinners, he said, *"Go thy way; from henceforth sin no more"* (Jn. 8:11).

Servants of the Lord have no authority from Christ to soften the demands of discipleship when they appear to work hardship on the lives of those who find themselves living in sin. The prostitute might have little other qualifications for supporting herself, the homosexual might burn in lust for one of his own kind, and the dishonest salesman may have a large family and find that his product will not sell legitimately. But all of them must cease to sin when they answer the call of the Lord.

What is the spiritual condition of companions who are divorced for reasons other than fornication and are remarried? Jesus said on two occasions: *"Whosoever shall put away his wife, except for fornication, and shall marry another, committeth adultery: and he that marrieth her when she is put away committeth adultery"* (Matt. 19:9; 5:32). The Lord says plainly they commit adultery. The preceding lesson contends that this truth applies to all men today and that disciples of the Lord must teach it as part of the new covenant. Jesus knew some could not receive this saying (Matt. 19:10-12). A growing number of brethren object to this view and their objections deserve analysis.

A Mosaic Law
Some brethren contend that what Jesus said is not a part of the gospel. They argue that he is answering a question of the Pharisees about the law of Moses and its regulations. They affirm that the *"except for fornication"* phrase is no part of the new covenant; that it was a part of the old covenant that Moses ignored because of the hardness of Israel's heart; that Jesus is merely reiterating to Jews God's original intention for Israel.

Does this view mean that only what is taught in the New Testament after Acts 2, when the church was established, applies to Christians? Surely not! How, for example, is a Christian to view the rest of Matthew 5, where Jesus taught no divorce and remarriage *"saving for the cause of fornication"* (v. 32)? There Jesus taught the beatitudes (vv. 1-12), letting one's light shine (vv. 13-16), and avoiding the sins of anger (vv. 21-24), adulterous lust (vv. 27,28), retaliation and hatred for enemies (vv. 38-48). Elsewhere in the gospels he taught faith, repentance, baptism, faithfulness, and a host of kingdom lessons in the parables (Matt. 28:18-20; Mk. 16:15,16; Lk. 24:45-49; 8:11-15; etc.).

These truths, it is said, are part of the new covenant because they are found also in Acts and the epistles. That argument fails for two reasons: (1) It admits that what Jesus taught in the gospels is part of the new covenant; (2) It assumes without proof that what Jesus taught in the gospels must be reaffirmed in the remainder of the New

Testament. Note also that the same *"but I say"* that Jesus used to condemn adulterous lust (Matt. 5:28) is used to teach *"saving for the cause of fornication"* (Matt. 5:32). How can one be binding on Christians and the other not?

But are those who object to "fornication" as the only cause for divorce and remarriage willing to accept what is taught in Acts and the epistles? There no exceptions are given at all. The apostle Paul affirms twice that husbands and wives are bound to one another so long as they live (see Rom. 7:2; 1 Cor. 7:39). This, if anything, strenghtens the case against the modern practice of divorce and remarriage for every cause. This leads to the next objection.

A Christian Law

Other brethren take an opposite view of the *"except for fornication"* phrase. They see Jesus as stating a law that applies only to Christians. What Jesus teaches has no reference to husbands and wives before they obey the gospel. Persons, they contend, may divorce and remarry 8 or 10 times without sin before they become Christians because they are not amenable to the law of Christ. As Paul wrote, *"Where there is no law, neither is there transgression"* (Rom. 4:15). Once couples obey the gospel, they are bound to one another till death and can divorce and remarry only on grounds of fornication. So the argument goes.

Who can dispute this? If unbelievers are not subject to Christ's law, then they cannot violate it. If they cannot violate it, they cannot be charged with sin. Sin is a transgression of law (1 Jn. 3:4) and cannot exist, as Paul says, *"where there is no law."* But what about the assumption that unbelievers are not responsible to the law of Christ? Since Christ is God's only spokesman for this age and since unbelievers, according to this objection, are not subject to his dictates, how can Paul say *"all have sinned"* and *"there is none righteous, no, not one"* (Rom. 3:23,10)? How can he call men sinners who are not subject to God's law for men today?

But Paul is more specific. To the Corinthians he wrote: *"Or know ye not that the unrighteous shall not inherit the kingdom of God? Be not deceived: neither fornicators, nor idolaters, nor adulterers, nor effeminate, nor abusers of themselves with men, nor thieves, nor covetous, nor drunkards, nor revilers, nor extortioners, shall inherit the kingdom of God. And such were some of you: but ye were washed, but ye were sanctified, but ye were justified in the name of the Lord Jesus Christ, and in the Spirit of our God"* (1 Cor. 6:9-11). The Corinthians were guilty of these sins as unbelievers — before they were washed and sanctified and justified by Christ. As unbelievers they were subject to the laws forbidding those deeds and were sinners.

But these laws, according to the objection, are not peculiar to the new covenant and antedate the law of Christ. They, it is affirmed, are universal laws that apply to all men and go back to the beginning. But that is true of the Lord's teaching on marriage! When the Pharisees noted that Moses granted divorces for every cause, Jesus replied, *"but from the beginning it hath not been so"* (Matt. 19:8). He had said previous to this that a man must leave his father and mother, must cleave unto his wife, and that what God hath joined together man must not put asunder (Matt. 19:5,6). The bond of marriage that cannot be put asunder except for fornication is not peculiar to the new covenant, but one stated by God at the first marriage (Gen. 2:24).

No one affirms that the sins listed by Paul and the teaching of Jesus on divorce and remarriage originated with the New Testament. It is true, however, that these ideas are a part of the gospel revealed to apostles and prophets by the Spirit (see Eph. 3:3-5). And Jesus said this gospel is to be preached to all nations and every creature (see Matt. 28:18-20; Mk. 16:15,16). All men are subject to this teaching to-day — not because it is taught from the beginning and not because it is in the law of Moses, but because it is in the gospel of Christ.

Baptism Washes Away Adultery

Some brethren readily acknowledge that the Lord's teaching on the permanence of marriage is a part of the gospel and that all men are amenable to it as law. They likewise agree that all couples who violate this law are sinners — adulterers! But they also contend that when these sinners are baptized their adultery is washed away, they are cleansed from all defilement, they are justified before God, and they are now permitted to continue the relationship free of transgression. The premise that baptism washes away sins is valid. No doubt about that at all (see Mk. 16:16; Acts 2:38; 22:16).

Notice, though, that baptism that washes away sins is preceded by repentance (Acts 2:38). Repentance, according to the teaching of John the Baptist, demands that one cease to sin. *"Bring forth therefore fruits worthy of repentance,"* he demanded (Lk. 3:8). To publicans repentance says stop cheating taxpayers (Lk. 3:13), to soldiers it demands wrongfully accusing no one (Lk. 3:14), and to Herod, who had his brother's wife and was living in adultery, it means to give her up for *"it is not lawful for thee to have her"* (Matt. 14:4).

The nature of repentance is not complicated. The thief, for example, ceases to steal, the drunkards stops getting drunk, the adulterer gives up his affairs, and the homosexual turns from his perverted lifestyle. The Corinthians, as noted, *"were"* all of these things, but gave them up because such people cannot inherit the kingdom of God (see 1 Cor. 6:9-11).

Husbands and wives are bound to one another so long as they live. Only death or divorce for fornication releases that tie. One who is divorced and joined to another for any other reason *"committeth adultery"* (Matt. 5:32; 19:9; Rom. 7:2). Baptism does not "untie" the first marriage and therefore does not eliminate the adultery. *"Committeth"* is present tense in Greek and means that adultery is a continual practice in an unlawful marriage. If an alien sinner can continue in an unlawful marriage after repentance without living in sin, then an erring Christian can continue in an unlawful marriage after repentance without living in sin! The same would apply to the guilty party — the fornicator — whether a believer or not. He could remarry, repent of his fornication, and continue in his unlawful marriage without sin. To rework a bit of old poetry: "Oh, what a tangled web men weave, When they follow teaching that men conceive."

It is mind boggling, according to this reasoning, to consider the polygamist. And since polygamy is still practiced, this is not merely hypothetical. What does a man who has four wives do? Does he stay with the last one and give up the first three? Or, does repentance and baptism legitimize all four marriages? To which one is he "bound" in God's eyes? God only joins one male and one female — the two become one flesh (Matt. 19:4,5). Any subsequent marriages after a man takes his first wife, except for fornication, are unlawful and forbidden while the first wife lives. They must be forsaken.

Abide In That Calling

But does not Paul say: *"Let each man abide in that calling wherein he was called"* (1 Cor. 7:20)? This means to some that one is to remain with whatever wife he has at the time he answers the call of the Lord to become a Christian. Just what did Paul have in mind?

The apostle, it is acknowledged, was speaking in this text of marriage. He was talking particularly to Christians who were joined to unbelievers. He tells them, first, to be content to dwell with them (v. 13). He notes, second, that the marriage is a legitimate one (v. 14). He observes, third, that by living with them they may save them (v. 16). He then concludes: *"Brethren, let each man, wherein he was called, therein abide with God"* (v. 24; also v. 20).

Paul illustrated the point by the examples of Jews, Gentiles, and slaves. If a man, for example, hears the gospel as a Jew, he should not seek to be uncircumcised. Or, as a Gentile, he should not seek to be circumcised. Circumcision or uncircumcision is nothing, he says. What really matters is keeping God's commandments (v. 18,19). The same is said to slaves. Rather than seeking their freedom, they should use their slavery to God's glory (vv. 21-23).

What Paul does not teach is that a man can abide in sin when he obeys the gospel. A man who is a thief, or a fornicator, or a drunkard is not counseled to abide in those states. So it is with one living in adultery. Paul does not say sin and immorality are "nothing." He does not say to "use" sin to the glory of God. He spoke in the context of a "sanctified" relationship between a Christian and an unbeliever (v. 14) — not an unholy relationship of one bound to a companion and living with another. The calling in which one is to abide may not be a condition or state of sin.

Conclusion

Both the Lord and the apostles spoke clearly and unequivocally about divorce and remarriage. Little room is left for misunderstanding the truth. Much space, however, is found in the hearts of all for emotions and feelings to interfere with accepting these views. The same can be said of baptism. That baptism is essential to salvation and that man is not justified by "faith only" is stated plainly (Acts 2:38; Jas. 2:24). But what about the man who suddenly dies as he is about to be baptized? Will he be saved? Feelings, emotions, sympathy want to say yes. But redemption is not based on how men may feel about it.

Those who insist that adulterous marriages be severed when one enters Christ are often thought to be calloused and uncaring. Some even call them "homewreckers." But men who so teach do it from deep convictions and loving devotion for the souls of men they believe to be in sin and in danger of damnation. They sometimes do it with tears streaming down their cheeks. No one denies the severity of Jesus' teaching to men of his own nation, but neither do they deny his love for their souls. When principle is involved, faithful teachers of God's word, as Nehemiah and Ezra (Ezra 10; Neh. 13), will insist that God's word be obeyed — even when it brings hardship to families.

An Outline Study Guide

Introduction:

A. What will judge men (John 12:48)? _____

_____

How costly is discipleship (Lk. 14:25,26,33; Matt. 19:16-22)? _____

_____

B. Summarize Jesus' teaching on divorce and remarriage (Matt. 5:31,32; 19:9).

_____

I. A Mosaic Law:

A. What evidence abounds in Matthew 5 to indicate Jesus is talking to kingdom citizens (vv. 1-16; 21-22; 27-28; 38-48)?_____

_____

B. What other ideas show that what Jesus taught personally applies to all men (Matt. 28:18-20; Mk. 16:15,16; Lk. 24:45-49; Lk. 8:11-15)?_____

_____

C. If Jesus speaks only to Jews in the gospels, may one then divorce and remarry for any reason (Rom. 7:2; 1 Cor. 7:39)? Explain._____

_____

II. A Christian Law:

A. What cannot exist where there is no law (Rom. 4:15)? _____

_____

What does Paul say about all men (Rom. 3:9,23)? _____

_____

B. What does 1 Corinthians 6:9-11 say about the New Testament's application to all men? _____

_____

Does the New Testament have universal application (Matt. 28:19; Mk. 16:15)?

_____

To whom was the original marriage law given and to whom did it apply (Gen. 2:24)?_____

_____

C. Who is God's spokesman today and who must hear him (Heb. 1:1,2; Matt. 17:5; Acts 3:22,23)? _____

_____

III. Baptism Washes Away Sins:

A. What do the Scriptures say about baptism washing away sins (Mk. 16:16; Acts 2:38; 22:16)? _____

_____

B. What precedes baptism (Acts 2:38)? _____

What does repentance demand one do about sin (Lk. 3:8,13,14; Matt. 14:4)?

_____

What does "were" indicate about the sins of the Corinthians (1 Cor. 6:11)?

_____

C. What two things "untie" a marriage (Matt. 19:9; 1 Cor. 7:39)? _____

_____

What must a polygamist do (Matt. 19:4,5)? _____

_____

IV. Abide In That Calling:
A. What does Paul say to Christians married to unbelievers (1 Cor. 7:20,24)?

_____

What three things does he say about these marriages (1 Cor. 7:13,14,16)?

_____

B. What three examples illustrate Paul's point about abiding (1 Cor. 7:18,19, 21-23)? _____

_____

What did he say to Jews?_____

_____

Gentiles? _____

Slaves? _____

C. May one abide in sin (see 1 Cor. 6:9-11)?_____

_____

What about homosexuals, thieves, drunkards, adulterers?_____

_____

Conclusion:
A. What is likely to interfere when one teaches on divorce and remarriage?___

_____

How is this same problem raised by denominational folks on baptism?_____

_____

B. How did Ezra and Nehemiah deal with emotions (Ezra 10 and Neh. 13)?___

_____

Ten Rules for Picking a Mate

Introduction

Nothing is quite as frustrating as talking to an 18 or 20 year old child about his choice of boy friend or girl friend, especially when that selection has been made for all the wrong reasons. Something many call "chemistry" develops between these youngsters and no amount of common sense can diffuse that oneness and rightness the two feel. And surely chemistry is important between a man and a woman, but feelings must not allow young people to ignore completely other important factors in picking a mate for life. Although talking to kids about mates may be like talking to a fence post or a brick wall, parents and older adults must not hesitate to issue a few warnings about the realities of what makes a good companion (see Eph. 6:1-4).

The "ten rules" suggested here were not delivered at Sinai, but it is believed that they pose serious questions that young people need to discuss before they finalize plans for marriage. Some of them merely note qualities to observe or look for in prospective mates. The "rules" are not intended to discourage marriage until young people find the "perfect" husband or wife. All happily married couples can testify to the change and growth that have been necessary to the success of their relationship. These guidelines can at least help weed out those who are totally unacceptable for marriage. Young folks are urged to come up for breath, release themselves from one another's arms, look beyond physical lust for a moment, and discuss frankly and sensibly what they really can offer one another in marriage.

These rules are included in this adult study guide for a couple of reasons. First, they contain principles that parents need to begin early to drill into the minds of their children. Second, they provide an excellent opportunity to review the principles of successful marriage. A number of the suggestions and points are but a repetition of ideas presented in previous lessons. They will, it is hoped, summarize in a short space much of what has already been said.

1. Pick a mate who respects God's word. God's way and the ways of the world have always been in conflict. God insists that man live by principles of righteousness (Acts 10:35) and the world follows the lust of the flesh, lust of the eyes, and pride of life (1 Jn. 2:15,16). The two are diametrically opposed to one another (Gal. 5:16-18). God demands that his people love not the world, deny themselves, and follow Christ (Lk. 9:23). The man of the world is at liberty to follow his sensual desires — even when it works hardship on others, including his wife. So it is with a woman of the world.

This difference creates practical problems when one of the mates is a Christian. What kind of leisure will the two engage in? Will he be satsified with a wife who will not put on a bikini and go to the beach with him on vacation? Will he be upset when she refuses to attend smutty movies? What kind of TV will he let the kids watch and what kind of language will he use before them? Will he drink, keep liquor in the house, get violent when he's had one too many? Oddly enough, these roles are reversed in many families, now that women "have come a long way, baby."

But it is not just a problem of morality. It is a problem of duties assigned by God. What about a man who does not accept his role as a husband and father to love and cherish his wife and children as his own body? What about a woman who rejects the duties of subjection, motherhood, and house-keeping? Couples must settle these important issues before marriage! Do they respect God's will for husbands, wives, fathers, mothers, or do they intend to find their own way in marriage — following their wisdom and lusts? The ways of the world have nothing good to offer marriage and young people better believe it now — before they take those vows (Eph. 5:22-33; 6:1-4; 1 Tim. 5:14; Tit. 2:3,4).

2. Pick a mate who has spiritual goals and values. Humanists have managed to incorporate what is called "values clarification" into the school systems. They love to pose situations in which students have to decide the value of one human over another. Ten people, for example, are on an island that can sustain only five of them. Determine, the kids are asked, which five are the most valuable and deserve to live. The other five, of course, must be murdered. The answer to this for Christians is simple. The value of persons is not assessed by material or physical worth and murder is wrong. But this is the catch. Humanists assert: man has no soul, value is estimated by temporal importance, there is no God, and murder in some situations is acceptable.

All of this is said not to discuss humanism per se, but to warn young people that success in marriage depends in measure whether companions have spiritual goals and values in life. Hollywood marriages, for instance, fail because the husband and wife lack these qualities. What is valuable to each is his career — not pleasing one another. Each, therefore, goes his separate way, ignoring the real worth and needs of the other. The same can be said of careers in the business world.

What is lacking is faith in God, belief that man is made in the image of God, and assurance that heaven is the goal of life on earth. Success in marriage is not possible when persons are viewed as thinking hunks of flesh that have only temporal, material value — and can be eliminated when they no longer further those goals. Husbands, wives, and children must be viewed as persons with supra-physical value, as souls who shine with spiritual beauty, as beings who deserve love, service, justice, and whatever sacrifice is necessary to supply them. Couples who think marriage can survive the materialistic values and goals of greed, lust, pleasure, and power are ignoring both the wisdom of God and the experience of man. Better check this out carefully, young people (Heb. 11:6; Gen. 1:26,27; Matt. 16:26; 1 Pet. 1:3-5).

3. Pick a mate who can adjust and compromise. No one is naive enough to think every possible difference between prospective couples can be anticipated in courtship. Once the two respect God and accept one another's real value, they readily seek to adjust and compromise within the guidelines God has set. That partners cannot know their companions until they live with them is not an old wives' tale. Many surprises will pop up in marriage and husbands and wives better be ready to shift gears in their thinking.

What is amazing in marriage is how much distress is ignited by the tiniest spark of irritation. Some wives can go bonkers over a husband's leaving his shorts in the middle of the bedroom floor. Or, a husband may climb the bathroom wall when his wife squeezes the toothpaste in the middle. Newlyweds are oblivious to the problems that grow out of clipping nails in the living room, chomping loudly or smacking lips while eating, failing to shower and shave daily, running tardy for appointments, leaving food-crusted plates on the end table, neglecting to pay bills promptly, snoring, letting the house get cluttered, allowing snack foods to deplete, and the list goes on.

The proverbial story of the man who divorced his wife for burning the toast or for eating crackers in bed is not as farfetched as unmarried folks would like to think. Adjustments and compromise are vital to happy marriages. What one mate refuses to correct, the other must accept. What one cannot accept, the other must correct. This kind of "give" and "take" is an integral part of the wedding game and young people need to assess it in their prospective mates (1 Cor. 13:4-7; Phil. 2:2-4).

4. Pick a mate who willingly corrects major flaws. As an extension of the previous rule, couples-to-be must work out major problems before they wed. Partners who refuse to correct flagrant flaws before marriage are less likely to change afterwards. It is folly to expect a mate who obeys not the gospel before the wedding to become a Christian a few weeks later. Unbelievers who assemble faithfully while the two are courting often quit altogether once the vows have been uttered. Sure there are exceptions, but do not count on it.

The same can be said of problems like drinking, gambling, nights out with the boys, and obsession with golf, fishing, or other sports. Despite promises to change, sinful habits or addictive pleasures will usually deepen as companions get more comfortable in the marriage. A look also at discourtesy, temper tantrums, unkindness, inability to face problems, physical abuse, lying, dishonesty, etc. is essential. Major character defects easily degenerate into intolerable living conditions. Beware, young people (1 Kgs. 19:1,2; 21:1-16).

5. Pick a mate who shows signs of maturity. The previous two rules are ways of saying that marriage is not for kids. That is why half of teenage marriages end in divorce. Maturity is a must. Kids are usually selfish and seek what is in their best interest. They are likely to be irresponsible and unable to look to the needs of others. This can be fatal to friendship with peers, but even more so to a permanent, intimate relationship like marriage. Successful marriage calls for duty above whim and personal pleasure.

If successful marriages have one secret, it is the indispensable quality of unselfishness. Companions must not enter marriage in search of happiness for themselves, but in pursuit of the delights of their mates. The ebb and flow of joy from partner to partner as they each seek the other's pleasure results from a mature approach to the relationship. "Marry to make your mate happy" is a simple rule that responsible adults understand and young people should discuss in advance of the wedding (Lk. 9:23; Matt. 23:11).

6. Pick a mate who can and will communicate. The joys of marriage are simple, uncomplicated, and basic, but can only be transmitted across communication lines. Husbands and wives cannot read one another's minds. What pleases a wife, as with God (1 Cor. 2:10,11), is a mystery to her husband until she reveals it. Her spirit must search out the deep things of her mind and make them known. What pleases her cannot be determined by the husband reasoning from the premise of what pleases him. She may love flowers, trinkets for a shadow box, or a crude homemade birthday card, but that is a far cry from a new tool, a box of computer disks, or a steak supper that turns him on. Knowing one another is essential to the joy of sex, mealtime delights, good times in a night out together, and a hundred other things (1 Pet. 3:7).

Communication is also necessary to solve problems. Problems are not settled by ignoring them. They call for thought, discussion, and mutually accepted solutions. Companions who will not express their feelings and openly criticize one another in love are neglecting "aggravations" that will fester and erupt. A wife who feels a need for more attention from her husband must open up those feelings for discussion. A husband who thinks his mother-in-law is dominating her daughter can ward off serious trouble by talking to his wife about it. A goal of courtship is to understand a prospective mate — an excellent time for young folks to determine whether they can bare their hearts to one another.

7. Pick a mate who can offer more than physical attractiveness. "Beauty is skin deep" is a fact that all humans rebel against. That men of all ages are leaving their wives for young beautiful women shows that it is not limited to youth. That handsome male strippers are now the rage among all ages of women demonstrates that even females have not escaped the lure of physical beauty. Think, therefore, how vulnerable teens and young adults are to this false standard for choosing a companion (Prov. 31:30).

All people in their sober moments know that no direct relationship exists between physical attractiveness and qualities for a successful marriage. Love, care, personality, maturity, unselfishness, thoughtfulness — even sexual prowess are not determined by the degree of bodily beauty in which they are wrapped. If they were, most of those Hollywood marriages would be rousing successes.

The fact is that handsome and beautiful prospects are often egotistical, self-centered people who think mostly of themselves. A physically attractive female may be more interested in how she appears in public, how she looks in her clothes, and how her makeup enhances her beauty. Beauties sometimes turn out to be "airheads" who seldom entertain a thought of someone else's well-being. So it is with those handsome hunks! As the warmth of a house at 20 degrees below zero is not based on the beauty of its architecture, so the warmth and intimacy of marriage do not rest on the great looks of the husband and the wife.

8. Pick a mate who knows the difference between sex and love. Society talks a lot about "making love" and usually means "having sex." It is a confused choice of terms and inappropriate reference that distorts the nature of love. Even animals, who know nothing of love, can have sex. That sex can be an expression of love no one disputes, but that "love" and "sex" are used synonymously is a grave injustice to anyone who cannot distinguish between the two. And this seems especially difficult for young folks to understand.

The union of two bodies as one flesh is sex. It can take place between a paying customer and prostitute, a couple of 14 year old kids, or a father and his daughter. It can happen in the back seat of an automobile, at a sleazy motel, or in a public park. And in none of these cases do the "bodies" have an interest in the emotional fulfillment, spiritual bonding, ongoing happiness, or total needs of the persons in the bodies. It is a mere hormonal happening to gratify physical lust — much like the gluttonous gobbling down of one's favorite meal (1 Cor. 6:16).

Love is not just important in marriage — it is absolute. Marriages are not surviving today because concern for the real person is absent between companions. The more husbands and wives care for the total being of one another, the more important each feels and the more energy and enthusiasm each contributes to the relationship. Sex is essential and vital to marriage. But only when it is perceived as one of many avenues of love can it be used properly to show tender affection for a mate to whom one is unselfishly dedicated. Better talk about these matters, young people (Eph. 5:25-29).

9. Pick a mate who is a good friend. A man's best friend should be his wife. And a woman's best friend should be her husband. Young people can determine this in their dates by taking a long hard look at how they spend their time. Are they constantly wrapped up in one another's arms? Or, do they spend long hours picnicing, sightseeing, visiting, and sharing in sporting events? Heavy petting, physical displays of affection, and lust may be fun, but they are seldom a good gauge of each other's personalities. When that ardor cools after a few weeks of marriage, the couple may look at each other across the table and decide they don't even like one another.

The key question for newlyweds and "oldlyweds" is whether they are good friends, whether they enjoy one another's company, whether they are close companions. Something, as already noted, can be said for "chemistry" and physical attraction, but the fact is that 95 percent of a couple's time together is consumed by matters other than sex. It can be a long boring life together, young people, if physical lust is the basis for the wedding. Give it some thought and make a commitment to someone who is fun to hang around with. Make certain those terms "boy friend" and "girl friend" have real meaning in those courting days (Acts 18:2,26; Rom. 16:3; 1 Cor. 16:19; 2 Tim. 4:19).

10. Pick a mate who views marriage as permanent. A person who buys a car to last for 20 years treats it differently than if he plans to trade every year. And so it is with the man or woman who marries a companion for life. Newlyweds who enter marriage with divorce as an option are not committed to the loving care that preserves relationships unto death. Obstacles to them become stumblingblocks rather than building blocks. The qualities, on the other hand, that couples develop to withstand the storms of life become the bonding elements that seal and protect the marriage against deterioration. Talking about problems, adjusting habits in the interest of peace, sacrificing to meet a need, and giving attention to little things are a few of those elements.

What God joins together man may not put asunder. Many prospective mates neither know nor believe that. More and more young folks come from broken homes and have no greater respect for the permanency of marriage than their parents had. Divorce tends to perpetuate itself in families. No longer can couples-to-be take for granted that their mate really means "unto death do us part." It is a topic that better be discussed thoroughly (Matt. 19:4-6; Rom. 7:2; 1 Cor. 7:39).

Conclusion
The principles laid down in this study, brethren, are not optional. They are the will and wisdom of God Almighty. They have been revealed from heaven for the happiness of the human family. At times they seem to be idealistic and beyond the reach of ordinary men. And maybe they are. After all, God intends to make extraordinary men by the power of the gospel of Christ. Men and women who will fill themselves with the dynamic energy of God's spiritual principles will find themselves unusually good husbands, wives, mothers, fathers, and children. No one denies the challenge God's word proposes for the family, but neither must any one deny the power available to meet that challenge. And think of the blessings it yields — the unspeakable joy and peace that fill the households of those who give and receive love after the likeness of Christ.

An Outline Study Guide
I. Respect For God:
  A. What does God demand (Acts 10:35; Lk. 9:23)? _____

  _____

  What does the world follow (1 Jn. 2:15,16)? _____

  _____

  B. List and discuss possible conflicts between husbands and wives when only one is a Christian. _____

  _____

II. Spiritual Values:
  A. What is "values clarification" and who promotes it? _____

  _____

  B. What are the basic values and goals of Christians (Heb. 11:6; Gen. 1:26,27; Matt. 16:26; 1 Pet. 1:3-5)? _____

  _____

  C. Why is it important for a Christian to marry someone who has the same values? _____

  _____

III. Adjustments and Compromise:
  A. Why can little matters become serious in marriage? _____

  _____

  B. How can love work to bring adjustments and compromise (Phil. 2:3,4; 1 Cor. 13:4-7)? _____

  _____

IV. Correcting Major Flaws:

A. What usually happens to major character flaws after marriage?_____

_____

B. What effect did Jezebel's character flaws have on her husband (1 Kgs. 19:1,2; 21:1-16)? _____

_____

V. Signs of Maturity:

A. Why do most teenage marriages end in divorce? _____

_____

B. What is a simple rule of marriage?_____

_____

What is the basis of successful marriages (Lk. 9:23; Matt. 23:11)? ____

_____

VI. Communications:

A. Along what lines are the joys of marriage transmitted? _____

_____

Cite examples. _____

_____

B. How are husbands to dwell with their wives (1 Pet. 3:7)? _____

_____

Does it work the other way?_____

_____

VII. Beyond Physical Attractiveness:

A. Explain and illustrate how physical beauty is a false standard._____

_____

B. How does the Bible state this (Prov. 31:30)?_____

_____

VIII. Love and Sex:

A. What clearly shows the difference between love and sex? _____

_____

B. Illustrate the difference biblically (1 Cor. 6:16; Eph. 5:25-29). _____

_____

C. How can sex be related to love (1 Cor. 7:1-6; Heb. 13:4)?_____

_____

IX. Good Friends:

A. Cite ways young people can tell if they are good friends. _____

_____ _____

B. Why is this necessary in marriage? _____

_____

X. Marriage Is Permanent:

A. What attitude do many newlyweds have when they enter marriage?___

_____

B. Summarize what the Scriptures say about the permanence of marriage (Matt. 19:6; Rom. 7:2; 1 Cor. 7:39). _____

_____